Never Too Late

Leveraging Technology
to Support
High School Readers
With Dyslexia

Yvonna Graham
and
Victoria Francis

Solution Tree | Press

Copyright © 2025 by Solution Tree Press

Materials appearing here are copyrighted. With one exception, all rights are reserved. Readers may reproduce only those pages marked "Reproducible." Otherwise, no part of this book may be reproduced or transmitted in any form or by any means (electronic, photocopying, recording, or otherwise) without prior written permission of the publisher. This book, in whole or in part, may not be included in a large language model, used to train AI, or uploaded into any AI system.

555 North Morton Street
Bloomington, IN 47404
800.733.6786 (toll free) / 812.336.7700
FAX: 812.336.7790

email: info@SolutionTree.com
SolutionTree.com
Visit **go.SolutionTree.com/literacy** to download the free reproducibles in this book.

Printed in the United States of America

Library of Congress Cataloging-in-Publication Data

Names: Graham, Yvonna, author. | Francis, Victoria (Teacher), author.
Title: Never too late : leveraging technology to support high school
   readers with dyslexia / Yvonna Graham, Victoria Francis.
Description: Bloomington, IN : Solution Tree Press, 2025. | Includes
   bibliographical references and index.
Identifiers: LCCN 2024043294 (print) | LCCN 2024043295 (ebook) | ISBN
   9781962188777 (paperback) | ISBN 9781962188784 (ebook)
Subjects: LCSH: Dyslexics--Education (Secondary) | Educational technology.
   | Reading--Technological innovations.
Classification: LCC LB1050.5 .G68 2025 (print) | LCC LB1050.5 (ebook) |
   DDC 371.91/443028--dc23/eng/20250120
LC record available at https://lccn.loc.gov/2024043294
LC ebook record available at https://lccn.loc.gov/2024043295

Solution Tree
Jeffrey C. Jones, CEO
Edmund M. Ackerman, President

Solution Tree Press
President and Publisher: Douglas M. Rife
Associate Publishers: Todd Brakke and Kendra Slayton
Editorial Director: Laurel Hecker
Art Director: Rian Anderson
Copy Chief: Jessi Finn
Production Editor: Madonna Evans
Copy Editor: Mark Hain
Text and Cover Designer: Julie Csizmadia
Acquisitions Editors: Carol Collins and Hilary Goff
Content Development Specialist: Amy Rubenstein
Associate Editors: Sarah Ludwig and Elijah Oates
Editorial Assistant: Madison Chartier

ACKNOWLEDGMENTS

My daughter didn't learn to read or write in first grade, but later she learned to read in a way that brought everything I thought I knew about reading into question. She taught me a hundred times more than I ever taught her about dyslexic thinking, brain science, music, mathematics, and life. She inspired and coauthored *Dyslexia Tool Kit: Expanded Edition* (2021), and created the cartoons in this book. Thank you, Alta!

I owe tremendous gratitude to my coauthor, Vicki Francis, who so skillfully adapted my tutoring techniques for use in her high school classroom, experimented tirelessly, and finally convinced me we had to get this information out to other teachers. She's the person who realized it's never too late for students with dyslexia.

My students with dyslexia of all ages have educated me in what works and what doesn't for neurodiverse learners—I am indebted to them and their parents for the chance to explore learning with so many delightful and creative young people.

Vicki and I wish to thank the extraordinary educators who read our early draft. They asked questions and offered insights that helped us speak more clearly and address a variety of classroom environments. Thank you to Ashley Januski, Barbara Cannon, Alta Graham, and Katie Williams!

The book in your hands is vastly better because of the Solution Tree teams of talented people! Huge thanks to editors Amy Rubenstein and Madonna Evans, the designers, and the publisher for seeing our vision even more clearly than we did. Thank you as well to the photographers for our author photos: Skye Davis and Brenda Leap.

—Yvonna

My journey in the world of dyslexia began in fourth grade when I started noticing that my brothers were struggling with reading. As we got older, I found it confusing that these intelligent, creative young men who could solve complex mechanical and technical problems were treated with disrespect in school, on the job, and even in their personal relationships because of their reading challenges.

It is why I became a teacher. I wanted to help.

I have much gratitude for my brother who, after a successful career as a diesel mechanic, had the courage and fortune to connect with a tutor who taught him not only how to overcome his dyslexia but also to have a new pride and confidence in his intelligence. I am grateful for the many hours that my brother spent educating me on what it is like to be dyslexic and how he advocates for himself. He answered many questions about the tools that he now uses to successfully navigate the written world. We've included those tools in this book so that you too can help others.

Along the journey, I befriended Yvonna, before her daughters were even born. Over the years, I watched her and her husband conquer so many challenges in providing a superior education for their daughters. She took that experience, along with her master's education, and developed tools

Visit **go.SolutionTree.com/literacy** to download the free reproducibles in this book.

and methods for tutoring students with dyslexia. She had a waiting list of parents desperate for help with their children. When I was asked to teach a high school English class of students who had failed the state test twice, Yvonna very graciously became the source and guidance for the tools that made a difference in my students' lives. I have so much gratitude and appreciation for her support.

Now we share these tools with you in hopes that having a better understanding of dyslexia, plus sample lesson plans and time-saving tips, will make it easier for you to reach those students who deserve respect and guidance to navigate the written world.

—Vicki

TABLE OF CONTENTS

Reproducibles are in italics

ABOUT THE AUTHORS xi

INTRODUCTION 1
    Dyslexia as a Hidden Superpower 3
    Dyslexia is More Prevalent Than You Think 6
    The Need for Classroom Tools 8
    About This Book 11
    Five Main Ideas 12
    What's in This Book 13
    Seeing Through the Invisibility Cloak 16

CHAPTER 1: USING TEXT-TO-SPEECH TOOLS 23
    What Text-to-Speech Is 24
    How Text-to-Speech Helps Students With Dyslexia ... 25
    Classroom Applications of Text-to-Speech 31
    How to Address Pushback From Naysayers 35
    Summary 37
    Sample Text-to-Speech Lesson Plan 40

CHAPTER 2: USING SPEECH-TO-TEXT TOOLS ... 49
- What Speech-to-Text Is ... 51
- How Speech-to-Text Helps Students With Dyslexia ... 52
- Classroom Applications of Speech-to-Text ... 55
- How to Address Pushback From Naysayers ... 59
- Summary ... 61
- *Sample Speech-to-Text Lesson Plan* ... 64

CHAPTER 3: TRACKING WITH AUDIO-ASSISTED READING ... 73
- What Tracking Is ... 75
- How Tracking Helps Students With Dyslexia ... 77
- Classroom Applications of Tracking ... 81
- How to Address Pushback From Naysayers ... 89
- Summary ... 90
- *Sample Tracking Lesson Plan* ... 93

CHAPTER 4: USING HEADPHONES AS AN EDUCATIONAL SUPPORT ... 103
- What Headphones Do ... 104
- How Headphones Help Students With Dyslexia ... 106
- Classroom Applications of Headphones ... 114
- How to Address Pushback From Naysayers ... 119
- Summary ... 121

CHAPTER 5: IMPLEMENTING RECORDED LESSONS ... 125
- What Recorded Lessons Are ... 126
- How Recorded Lessons Help Students With Dyslexia ... 127
- Classroom Applications of Recorded Lessons ... 133
- How to Address Pushback From Naysayers ... 139
- Summary ... 141
- *Common IEP and 504 Goals That Lesson Recording May Meet* ... 143

CHAPTER 6: UNDERSTANDING THE
IMPACT OF ARTIFICIAL INTELLIGENCE **147**
    What Artificial Intelligence Is 149
    The Vocabulary of AI 151
    How Artificial Intelligence Helps Students With Dyslexia . . . 154
    Classroom Applications of Artificial Intelligence 157
    How to Address Pushback From Naysayers 162
    Summary 164
    Reflection 165
    Accommodations for Students With Dyslexia
    That AI Can Help Meet 166

EPILOGUE **169**

APPENDIX **173**
    Lesson Plan Template 174

REFERENCES AND RESOURCES **181**

INDEX **191**

ABOUT THE AUTHORS

 **Yvonna Graham, MEd,** started her career in education in the 1980s at an alternative high school in Las Cruces, New Mexico, where experience convinced her that literacy is crucial for breaking failure cycles. When her daughter struggled with severe dyslexia, Graham pursued a master's degree focusing on research-based reading instruction and homeschooled her daughter. These methods so successfully impacted her daughter's reading ability that Graham went from hearing a teacher predict that her daughter would be lucky if she could "learn to wipe tables" to watching her earn four college degrees, including a doctorate in music composition and a master's in computer science. Graham self-educates continually about neurodiversity in education. She is passionate about literacy, and actually enjoys reading research papers.

Knowing that her methods could help other students with dyslexia, Graham started Mumbling Marmot Tutoring in Durango, Colorado, where her clientele grew so much that she began hiring and training tutors for kindergarten through college students. Her interest in sharing the methods more widely resulted in her first book, *Dyslexia Tool Kit: What to Do When Phonics Isn't Enough, Expanded Edition* (self-published, 2021).

Graham feels especially honored to have been interviewed by three of her literacy heroes: Marion Blank (Reading Kingdom, author of *The Reading Remedy*), Fernette Eide (coauthor of *The Dyslexic Advantage*), and Sam Bommarito, the featured speaker at LitCon 2022. The interviews are available on YouTube.

Graham received a bachelor of arts degree in psychology from Evangel University in Springfield, Missouri, and a master's degree in special education with a focus on neurodiversity from the University of New Mexico in Albuquerque.

Graham enjoys blogging about dyslexia at www.dyslexiakit.net and leading workshops for teacher and parent groups, as well as private consulting with parents of students with dyslexia.

Victoria Francis, MEd, EdS, spent forty years teaching high school English, newspaper, yearbook, photography, and graphic design classes in Idaho, New Mexico, and Hawaii. Overseeing a thirty-computer Mac lab and an award-winning publications program at Capital High School in Boise, Idaho, her focus was providing opportunities to develop skills that would launch students into successful jobs after graduation. Along with watching family members struggle with dyslexia, it was during her first teaching job in 1981 at an alternative high school in Las Cruces, New Mexico that Francis developed a passion for working with "underdog"

students—those who others felt had poor future prospects. She saw their strengths beyond their disabilities and worked to help them see the same.

Francis has served on numerous curriculum and standards development committees, including writing state and district journalism and photography curricula. After obtaining National Board Teaching Certification in Career and Technical Education (CTE), she was invited to critique portfolios at the national and state levels. Believing that travel is a great educator, over the years Francis took hundreds of students to journalism conferences in cities across the United States.

Trained by Fredric Jones, Francis taught classes in his classroom management training program to district- and state-level teachers. Using his methods, she established the behavioral and instructional foundation in her classroom that enabled her to easily incorporate the methods described in this book.

Francis received a bachelor of science degree in journalism and English education from New Mexico State University in Las Cruces, a computer specialist master of education degree from Lesley University in Cambridge, Massachusetts, and an education specialist degree in curriculum and instruction with an emphasis on CTE administrative certification from the University of Idaho. After retirement, she pursued her passion for quilting, began a quilting business, and is working toward an international quilt-judging certification.

INTRODUCTION

> I think the first thing is to help teachers to understand dyslexia . . . because there are one in five kids in every classroom that are dyslexic. So every teacher is a teacher of dyslexic children.
> —KATE GRIGGS

We started our journey as educators at an alternative high school in the early 1980s. We were part of an experiment to see if students who had dropped out or been expelled could be helped. Our school accepted one hundred students, all of whom had dropped out of high school. Some students had been in jail, some needed to work to support themselves, and some were pregnant. Pregnant students were not allowed to attend high school at that time.

We taught a few structured classes, but most of the instruction was in small groups or one-on-one. Each student worked with a staff member to devise an individualized path to graduation or GED passage. Students were allowed to test out of material they already knew.

The halls were lined with charts showing each student's progress toward their goal, and students loved filling in another square on their chart when they finished a unit. Students' schedules were adjusted to accommodate work hours, childcare availability, and other needs.

Some students who were good readers flourished with independent study, but students who struggled with reading tended to need more support. We were able to adjust our curriculum to match the student need as long as we met state standards. So, we minimized the amount of required reading for these students, as we didn't yet have the technology that allows struggling readers to fully participate in a text.

That experience informed how we approached our students for the rest of our careers. When we left that school for other jobs, we took with us the deep conviction that a great deal of academic failure is tied to literacy—but we didn't yet know what to do about high school students who couldn't read. At that point, we didn't understand what dyslexia was or how it impacted our students.

Vicki went to work at a medium-sized public high school teaching journalism and photography. She encountered students who, like her three brothers, had dyslexia and struggled to succeed in high school despite their intelligence and creativity. Yvonna, responding to her daughter with dyslexia, built a career as a dyslexia tutor while devouring research on this learning difference and developing ways to apply the research with individual students.

Our educational journeys converged again years later when Vicki realized she could take the research-based techniques that were successful in Yvonna's one-on-one tutoring and adapt them for high school classrooms. At the same time, technology-based audio and text tools were becoming widely available.

With the advent of audiobook access, speech-to-text, and text-to-speech, we realized that students with dyslexia no longer needed to rely on a peer reader or parent. Technology made it possible to offer tools to high school students to help them improve their reading ability outside of school and teacher time. Yvonna's one-on-one techniques were now adaptable for high school students both in and out of the classroom.

We wrote this book because we realized that most high school teachers never have a chance to witness what new technology can do for students who struggle with dyslexia, as this isn't part of their training. We want to share what we've learned so that students with dyslexia and their teachers can experience joyful learning rather than frustration.

This book is a fusion of dyslexia research, high school classroom experience, and technological advances. We hope it sparks hope and excitement for you and your students, as it has for us. Don't fear if you don't happen to be a digital native. You don't need to be a technology expert to use the tools in this book. There are now tech tools available for free on computers and phones that *can* open doors for your students with dyslexia.

You can be sure that you have students with dyslexia in your classroom, because an estimated 20 percent of the U.S. population is dyslexic (Yale Center for Dyslexia & Creativity, n.d.b). All you need to do to help these students is be open to the possibilities and give permission to explore them. Your students will take it from there.

Dyslexia as a Hidden Superpower

Do you remember not being able to read? For you, assuming you don't have dyslexia, words on a page are most likely flat, and nothing moves as you read except your eyes. This makes reading smooth, nearly magical. The meaning happens instantly in the brain without even having to think about the words.

The magic in brains with dyslexia is different! Readers with dyslexia have told us they see words flowing into each other like water, or spinning like tops, or words that look like segmented bricks. This is hard for a neurotypical person to imagine.

Although they struggle to read, people with dyslexia see connections, relationships, and patterns that others may miss. Dyslexia researchers Brock L. Eide and Fernette F. Eide (2023), authors of *The Dyslexic Advantage: Unlocking the Hidden Potential of the Dyslexic Brain*, explain that some of the most interesting data come from Manuel Casanova, professor of biomedical sciences at the University of South Carolina School of Medicine. Casanova found that bundles of neurons in our brains, called minicolumns, are arranged differently in individual brains. Eide and Eide (2023) provide an overview of Casanova's findings:

> Some brains contained tightly packed minicolumns while in other brains the minicolumns were more loosely spaced. In the human population as a whole, minicolumn spacing forms a bell-shaped or normal distribution. In most people this spacing is close to an average value, while a smaller number of people have minicolumns that are either more widely or more tightly spaced. When [Casanova] looked more closely at the "tails" of the distribution, he found something interesting. As he told us, "When we looked at the end of the spectrum that was characterized by widely spaced minicolumns, we found a very high proportion of individuals with dyslexia. Not surprisingly, when we looked, we found a high proportion of individuals with autism in the other tail of minicolumn spacing, where the minicolumns are closely packed.". . . Brains with more widely spaced minicolumns sent out larger axons that formed physically longer-distance connections, creating larger circuits and involving more distant parts of the brain. Longer connections, like those enriched in dyslexic brains, are poorer at fine-detail processing but excel at recognizing large features or concepts—that is, at big-picture tasks. . . . Circuits formed from such long connections are also useful for tasks that require problem-solving—especially in new or changing circumstances—though they are slower, less efficient, and less reliable for familiar tasks and less skilled in discriminating fine details. (pp. 44–45)

The research by Casanova and Eide and Eide (2023) is fascinating because it begins to explain how people with dyslexia can be brilliant in complex fields such as mechanics, computer science, and music theory while failing to learn to read. Their brains are wired for finding connections between ideas that seem unrelated and for noticing patterns in large amounts of data, but not for rote memorization or the fine details of printed text. Dyslexic thinking often sparks great inventors, artists, and entrepreneurs—think Leonardo da Vinci, Albert Einstein, or Richard Branson, who all likely had dyslexia (Eide & Eide, 2023).

For those wanting to dive deeper into dyslexic brain structure, mathematics educator Jennifer Plosz (n.d.) provides highly detailed and beautiful diagrams illustrating Casanova and colleagues' findings. Figure I.1 shows her artistic rendering of this feature of their research.

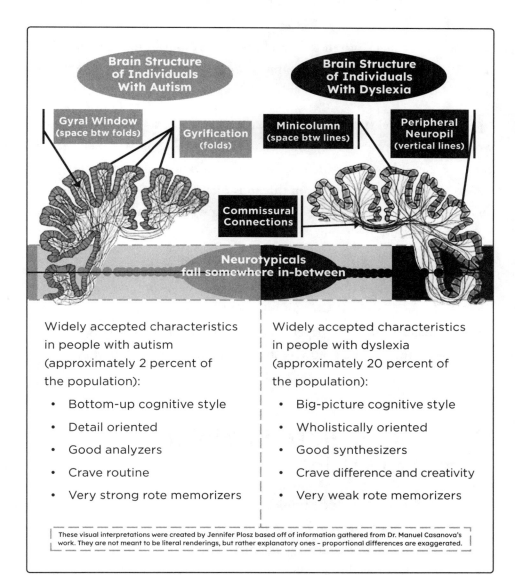

Source: Plosz, n.d.

Figure I.1: Dyslexia and autism differences in brain structure.

Because of these structural differences in dyslexic brains, dyslexic thinking can be a marvelous advantage, but not when learning to read. For example, Eddie, an auto mechanic with dyslexia, sees in his mind the inside of the car's engine in 3-D, enabling him to diagnose problems. In fact, he said that he is better than a heart surgeon because he can "bring his patients back from the dead!" However, when it comes to reading, he also sees each letter in a word in 3-D, and the letters "spin." This explains why he has been known to write his name as *Ebbie* instead of *Eddie*. The *d* and *b* will flip in his brain.

Some people with dyslexia describe letters crawling around like ants or words switching places. They may see the word as a whole or a picture and can't see that it has any parts. Readers with dyslexia experience text in a variety of ways, but the common thread is that it takes an extraordinary amount of mental energy to read by decoding words (Yale Center for Dyslexia & Creativity, n.d.c).

This information about dyslexic brains is crucial for high school teachers as it provides insight into why students may exhibit creativity, high intelligence, and a marvelous sense of humor, yet refuse to read an assignment or turn in a paper. In this book, we offer tech tools that can improve the potential of these students without sacrificing more teacher time.

Dyslexia is More Prevalent Than You Think

Because readers with dyslexia think much faster than they read, they tend to get bogged down. Comprehension suffers. A thirty-minute homework assignment for many of your students may take several stressful hours for one with dyslexia, if they can finish at all. Consequently, you may be frustrated and confused when students who seem smart and articulate refuse to hand in assignments. Though there can be many reasons for this, a distinct possibility is a reading problem, whether diagnosed or not.

As we established, dyslexic brains are typically creative. They find multiple ways to distract teachers and peers from the monumental difficulties they face in the classroom. By high school, many students with dyslexia give up on being successful in the school environment. Instead, they try to gain some self-esteem by becoming the class clown or finding ways to distract the other students. In our experience, by the time they get to high school, students with dyslexia are often masters of disguise and have expert methods of making their inability to read invisible to others.

When a high school student is creative and inventive but makes excuses for not turning in written work, consider the question: Might it be dyslexia? There are a variety of things that could explain this behavior, including other neurodiversities. But while many schools provide support for students with attention-deficit/hyperactivity disorder (ADHD) or autism spectrum disorder (ASD), we see a distinct lack of resources that help teachers better support their students with dyslexia.

With the tools in this book, you can provide a path for students that allows them a chance to use their strengths instead of being judged on their perceived weaknesses. But first we need to identify these students.

Not only do high school students with dyslexia try to hide their difficulty reading, but schools also tend to avoid dealing with it. A global research effort spearheaded by Made by Dyslexia (2022), an organization led by people with dyslexia to educate and empower others with dyslexia, reveals that 80 percent of students with dyslexia leave school undiagnosed. Some other interesting findings from the study include the following.

- Only one in ten teachers has a good understanding of dyslexic thinking.
- Over half of teachers say their school fails to understand dyslexic challenges.
- Only 4 percent of schools screen *all* learners for dyslexia (Made by Dyslexia, 2022).

The Made by Dyslexia school findings highlight the need for teachers to have ready tools to assist students with dyslexia, even though most of those students will likely be undiagnosed.

Let's lower the invisibility cloak that too often surrounds students with dyslexia, leaving them unseen and unsupported. We don't recommend a push for diagnosis. That's not a high school teacher's responsibility. But let's support struggling readers however we can.

Unfortunately, the stance of most high schools is that reading instruction is the responsibility of elementary educators and that nothing more can be done. We obviously disagree. However, most high schools do not offer help for dyslexia other than standard accommodations, such as longer time on tests. They do not address the actual reading problem. We simply want teachers to be aware of the students in their classrooms who can benefit dramatically when they introduce certain tech tools.

Would you like to see through the invisibility cloak to get an idea of how many students with dyslexia hide in your classes? Would you like to discover more about who they are beyond your classroom? At the end of this chapter, you'll find a reproducible tool, "Seeing Through the Invisibility Cloak" (page 16), that guides you through a simple process to answer these questions. We recommend you use this before you dig into the other classroom tools we present throughout this book.

The Need for Classroom Tools

I (Vicki) was happily teaching high school yearbook, newspaper, and photography classes when my principal told me he was giving one of my photography classes to another teacher so I could teach a special new English class that had been mandated by the state. It was a high-stakes class for senior students who had twice failed the state graduation test.

I would be teaching grammar—to seniors who probably hated English class. All were poor readers, due to many factors. They were in their last semester of high school. Despite whatever grades they had in other classes or their GPA, since they had failed the state test, they had to pass my class to graduate.

Two very fortunate things happened.

First, I realized that I had freedom to develop the course exactly how I wanted. These students did not have to take the state test ever again. This meant that I could start from their skill level and proceed from there rather than getting them ready for some other state-level or benchmark assessment or future class. Also, I had no curriculum, no books, and no support. I was not allowed to see the state test to find out what they had "failed." Instead of feeling deflated, I took it as permission to develop the coursework from scratch.

Second, it didn't take long for me to recognize that, generally, the students learning English as an additional language seemed eager and ready to work, while most other students were reluctant, angry, and frustrated. Why? I knew they were bright, intelligent people, but they had been unmotivated in prior English classes, and most, historically, did not turn in work, exhibited challenging behaviors, and skipped classes. All these factors made me suspect dyslexia might be a contributing factor for some of these students. I wondered if there was something I could do for them.

I grew up with such students in my family. My three brothers each had dyslexia and exhibited the same behaviors as they struggled through English classes, despite having exceptional skills in mechanics, computers, and art. They, too, would have been angry to be assigned to such a high-stakes class their senior year. I knew that anger and resistance in class were signals for me to show patience, speak softly and confidently, and treat them with respect.

As I pulled out the individualized education plans (IEPs) and 504 plans and looked at the drop-down menus on the attendance lists, I was able to see which students had a dyslexia diagnosis. I knew other students almost certainly dealt with the same challenge but were undiagnosed.

I then consulted the book *Dyslexia Tool Kit: What to Do When Phonics Isn't Enough*, by my coauthor, Yvonna Graham, and her daughter Alta E. Graham (2021). Even though many of the tutoring tools in the book were best suited for elementary students, there were a few gems that fit my needs perfectly. Technology tools such as speech-to-text were readily available as part of Google Classroom, and audiobooks were available in the school library. Best of all, these tools didn't require a big time investment, which was something I didn't have to give. After multiple phone calls to Yvonna, I began adapting methods from *Dyslexia Tool Kit* to support the students in my classroom.

Not wanting to embarrass the students with dyslexia or make the other students think that tech tools were only for those with dyslexia, I presented them as strategies we were all going to use, never indicating that I was targeting the students with dyslexia. As a result, everyone in the class benefited, including the students learning English.

I taught the class how to use each tool, step by step. We practiced together. And, surprisingly, it didn't take long before they were learning grammar using their new tools, with little prompting from me.

Once the tools were a normal part of the everyday structure of the class and everyone was smoothly working on the lessons, I explained to the entire class what dyslexia was and how the tools could help with it and other reading challenges. I also pointed out to everyone that, statistically, they may one day be working with someone who is dyslexic and it would be to their advantage to understand what it is and how the tools could help. By then, all students were whole-heartedly using the tools, not concerned with who might be dyslexic or why I had introduced them.

Even though I never sought out the students with dyslexia or referred to them specifically, I wanted both the students with dyslexia and those without to understand why we were using the tools and how those tools could support them.

The most heart-warming moments came as students visited with me quietly after class to reveal that they knew or suspected they had dyslexia. They said that the tech tools helped them quickly and correctly fill out job applications. One student was so excited about the methods that he brought in his old, battered laptop and pleaded with me to help him get the apps loaded onto the machine. A few days later, he boasted about turning in an English paper that week in another class. He said that normally it would take him hours to do a paper and that many times he just didn't turn it in. He beamed when he said the paper only took two hours, and it was quality work he was proud to turn in.

At that point, I knew that I somehow needed to share these tools with other teachers. I started talking to Yvonna about writing a book specifically for high school teachers using my adaptations of her methods.

About This Book

This book is for high school teachers who want to make their classrooms more inviting, effective, and inclusive for students with dyslexia without sacrificing teacher time or subject content. It also provides information to help you meet the demands and pressures from administrators to show how these tools can help meet standards as well as IEP and 504 accommodations.

Of these two types of accommodation, 504 plans are for students with disabilities who need adjustments to the learning environment to help meet their needs in the classroom. This is different from an IEP, which includes specialized instruction to help students learn the material.

A 504 plan is a bit less involved and formal than an IEP, which requires a comprehensive evaluation and lists very specific goals and services (Schultz, 2022). Teachers are required to provide accommodations and individualized instruction as directed in IEPs and 504 plans. The tech tools in this book will make compliance easy and effective.

If meeting all these requirements sounds impossible, please keep reading.

The purpose of this book is to provide high school teachers with information about the kinds of digital tools they can use to help students with dyslexia access the same information as their peers and perhaps even learn to read well. It includes examples of how to use these tools in the classroom and easy-to-use reproducibles to help you implement the ideas right away.

We wrote this book to share our experiences in adapting the research-based techniques dyslexia tutors use in high school classrooms. Because of the proliferation of students with dyslexia and other reading challenges, every high school teacher needs this information, regardless of subject area. We want to share what we've learned about fully including students with dyslexia. We believe that, if teachers have the right tools, they will naturally use those tools to help all their students succeed.

We have intentionally used short paragraphs and added white space in this book to make it easier for people with dyslexia to read. As teachers and administrators may also struggle with dyslexia, we want the text to be as accessible as possible.

Additionally, we aim to set an example of making small adjustments, such as increasing white space, that can help readers keep their place and reduce the visual distortions that readers with dyslexia experience (British Dyslexia Association, n.d.). Also know that we changed personal names in this book to protect privacy. Each chapter also features dyslexia-themed comics by Alta E. Graham.

Five Main Ideas

There are five central ideas behind this book.

1. Dyslexia *is* a high school challenge, as much as it is a challenge in all grades. Literacy challenges don't go away after elementary school, even for many students who have had appropriate intervention.

2. Every teacher has students with dyslexia in their classes.

3. High school teachers have neither the time nor training to teach reading.

4. Technological advances have opened a wonderful new path for students with dyslexia and for their teachers. However, the ways to use these tech tools effectively aren't always obvious.

5. Using technology to pave the way to academic success for students with dyslexia benefits *all* students while saving time for teachers.

It's never too late to extend hope and help to a student with dyslexia. Using technology available on any smartphone or computer, alongside a subtle but powerful shift in handling assignments, can change any classroom from toxic to triumphant for students who struggle to read.

What's in This Book

Each chapter in the book describes a tech tool that can help students with dyslexia reach their academic potential while, at the same time, benefit all students and ease the workload for teachers. You can read the chapters in order or choose which one is most useful to you at any given time.

- **Chapter 1: Using Text-to-Speech Tools**—Complex sentences cannot be understood by slowly sounding out one word at a time. Thankfully, there's a solution. Students can use text-to-speech apps to listen to reading assignments. This can help students with dyslexia fully participate in the classroom.

- **Chapter 2: Using Speech-to-Text Tools**—Students with dyslexia may be highly skilled in verbal language but can find putting words on paper nearly impossible. Furthermore, the poor quality of their own written work may make them avoid handing it in. Speech-to-text technology allows students with dyslexia to produce high-quality writing more easily.

- **Chapter 3: Tracking With Audio-Assisted Reading**—You can't teach struggling students how to read while also teaching mathematics, history, biology, or even English literature. But you can give them the tools they need to improve their reading and succeed in school and career. Tracking with a finger or eyes while listening to the text read aloud is the most powerful tool in this book. It may also be the most overlooked tool in high school professional development. This tool uses audiobooks and text *together* and involves active student participation, thus allowing students with dyslexia to build reading vocabulary while learning the same material as the rest of the class. Best of all, practicing this tool can benefit every student in your class.

- **Chapter 4: Using Headphones as an Educational Support**—Our world is crowded. Noise and overstimulation constantly distract some students with dyslexia while, ironically, some students with dyslexia need sound (such as specific types of music) to concentrate. School classrooms can make focus very challenging. Headphones make it bearable. It should not require an IEP or 504 for a student to use such a basic tool. Many professionals routinely use headphones when they need to concentrate. It's reasonable to let students with dyslexia use headphones during independent work.

- **Chapter 5: Implementing Recorded Lessons**—Use of a recording device allows students with dyslexia to replay lessons to clarify understanding of directions or concepts. Since multiple students may benefit from having a recorded lesson, it makes sense for the teacher to record the lesson rather than for several students to record from their desks.

- **Chapter 6: Understanding the Impact of Artificial Intelligence**—Teachers may feel concerned that students can easily use generative artificial intelligence (AI) programs such as ChatGPT and its competitors to write papers or do homework. While there are certainly problematic aspects to AI in the classroom, AI programs may also prove to be the most powerful tech tools ever invented. We discuss embracing them instead of banning them. Happily, teachers can use AI to further empower students with dyslexia while easing the paperwork load for themselves.

To enable you to use the chapters independently of each other, they all follow the same structure, as follows.

- **Description:** This part of the chapter introduces and explains the tool, describing what it is and what it does.

- **Research:** This part provides an overview of the science that supports using this tool for dyslexia.

- **Classroom:** This part advises you on practical application of the tool, including time saving tips for teachers.

- **Pushback:** This part helps you prepare for naysayers who may stand in the way of your work.

- **Summary:** Finally, the summary provides a quick recap of the chapter, including reflection questions and any reproducible tools.

Many educators haven't considered using tech tools that can efficiently and inexpensively help students with dyslexia succeed. By the time you finish this book, you will be much better informed. You will know how to respond to challenges in a way that works while being respectful of all your students.

Small shifts can turn your classroom into a place where every student, regardless of current reading ability, is fully included. These often overlooked approaches can make your job easier at the same time. Your students with dyslexia can now benefit from fully inclusive teaching that meets not only essential learning standards but IEP and 504 goals as well. Your most creative students can be leaders instead of distractors, and your job can be more rewarding.

REPRODUCIBLE

Seeing Through the Invisibility Cloak

This short three-part exercise will allow you to understand which of your students may be dyslexic and how many are in each class.

Part 1: Get to Know Your Class

1. How many students do you currently have in all classes?

   _____
   _____
   _____
   _____

2. Identify the students in your classes who have been diagnosed with dyslexia. You can check by looking for this diagnosis in your students' IEPs and 504 plans. Which of your students have been diagnosed? Please write their names here.

   _____
   _____
   _____
   _____

3. How many of your students have a dyslexia diagnosis?

   _____
   _____
   _____
   _____

4. Divide the total number of students identified as dyslexic by your total class load. For example, fifteen identified students divided by a class load of 150 students yields 0.10 or 10 percent of your total students. What percentage of students identified as dyslexic do you have?

   _____
   _____
   _____
   _____

page 1 of 5

Never Too Late © 2025 Solution Tree Press • SolutionTree.com
Visit **go.SolutionTree.com/literacy** to download this free reproducible.

REPRODUCIBLE | 17

5. Statistically, one in five people, or about 20 percent of the population, has dyslexia (Yale Center for Dyslexia & Creativity, n.d.). Multiply the total number of students in your class load by 0.20. For example, 150 total students times 0.20 equals thirty students who statistically would be likely to exhibit dyslexia. Estimated number of students with dyslexia in your class:

_____
_____
_____
_____
_____

6. How does the identified percentage compare to the estimated percentage?

_____
_____
_____
_____
_____

7. What do these percentages tell you?

_____
_____
_____
_____
_____

8. How many undiagnosed students may be in your classes?

_____
_____
_____
_____
_____

Part 2: Get to Know Your Students Identified With Dyslexia

It's important to start understanding who your students with dyslexia really are and appreciate the complexity of dyslexia. Not surprisingly, students with dyslexia often have poor grades in academic classes yet excel in art, music, and career and technical classes. By looking at their performance in other classes, you may instantly gain insight into where your students' strengths lie and begin to understand who they are as people.

Noting when students excel in some classes and fail in others is an excellent way to start identifying possible dyslexia, because some classes require extensive reading and others are more hands-on. Furthermore, recognizing students' strengths goes a long way toward connecting with students who may feel misunderstood by teachers.

Make a list of all the identified students who have been diagnosed with dyslexia in your classes. Check their grades in other classes. Next to their name, list the classes with the highest grades and lowest grades.

Diagnosed Students	Classes With the Highest Grades	Classes With the Lowest Grades

Part 3: Get to Know Your Students Unidentified With Dyslexia

We know students with dyslexia are sitting in our classrooms, but they can still be hard to spot. Here's a great way to discover who they might be.

REPRODUCIBLE

Make a list of students who struggle in your classes even though they seem academically capable of doing the work. Look at their grades in other classes and record them below.

Undiagnosed Students	Classes With the Highest Grades	Classes With the Lowest Grades

Never Too Late © 2025 Solution Tree Press • SolutionTree.com
Visit **go.SolutionTree.com/literacy** to download this free reproducible.

1. What do you notice?

   _____
   _____
   _____
   _____
   _____
   _____
   _____
   _____
   _____
   _____

2. Are there any similarities or differences between these identified and unidentified students?

   _____
   _____
   _____
   _____
   _____
   _____
   _____
   _____
   _____
   _____

References

Yale Center for Dyslexia & Creativity. (n.d.). *See what learners are saying about overcoming dyslexia on Coursera!* Accessed at www.dyslexia.yale.edu/learner-reviews on December 15, 2024.

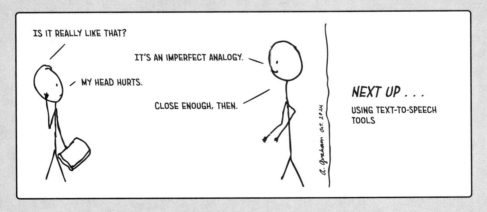

CHAPTER 1

Using Text-to-Speech Tools

*My dyslexic thinking means
I don't just think outside the box. . . .
I think outside the planet!*
—MAGGIE ADERIN-POCOCK

Behaviors such as skipping class or sleeping through class may signal despair rather than rebellion. Giving frustrated students the tools they need to learn more about their deepest interests can change their trajectory. When thinking about a sullen struggling reader in the back row, consider the story of Maggie Aderin-Pocock. Although she felt unhappy and disconnected in school due to her dyslexia, a passionate interest in science provided the motivation to help her overcome her challenges:

> The now celebrated space scientist, mechanical engineer, and science communicator grew up bouncing from one area of the country to another, the child of two Nigerian immigrants who divorced when she was young. She went to 13 different schools before she was 18 years old. Diagnosed with dyslexia at the age of eight, young Maggie started out hating school. "It didn't agree with me. . . . I used to sit at the back of the classroom and sort of skulk a bit. Because of my dyslexia, my reading and writing weren't very good at all." (Yale Center for Dyslexia & Creativity, n.d.a)

Although Maggie's prospects didn't look good for much of her school life, she had been absorbing information all along. Growing up, Maggie pretended to sleep in school because she hated going to class. She felt ostracized because of her dyslexia and thought she wasn't as smart as her peers. Then, she discovered her knack for science. Slowly, Maggie's confidence began to grow as her father helped foster her newfound interest. He took her to the library, checked out physics and astronomy books, and studied them with her (DyslexiaHelp, n.d.a).

Maggie's father provided the bridge she needed to build vocabulary and background knowledge, which allowed her to pursue her interest in science. This can make all the difference for students with dyslexia, even those not lucky enough to have a parent who wants to study physics with them. Text-to-speech technology makes positive change possible for students who may seem beyond reach.

In the rest of this chapter, we'll reveal how students with dyslexia can use text-to-speech not only to access their classroom reading assignments but also feed their hunger for knowledge in any field, with or without a parent to read with them.

What Text-to-Speech Is

Text-to-speech is an assistive technology that reads digital text aloud. It's sometimes called *read-aloud technology*. Text-to-speech software turns printed text into audio.

Dozens of apps are available to do this, but most schools now provide Google Classroom or similar platforms on all school computers for use by staff and students, and these include the option of turning on text-to-speech.

Text-to-speech has become a widely used technology in online reading tutor companies, such as Reading Rockets (n.d.b), that cater to learners with dyslexia. However, high schools have been slow to adapt and adopt this technology to assist students and teachers.

Text-to-speech technology in the classroom may help students to do the following.

- Access audiobooks for class reading assignments
- Turn class notes into audio files for study
- Have test and homework questions read aloud in real time without involving a human reader
- Have text read aloud in a language other than English
- Read and comprehend at their intellectual level rather than their reading level
- Hear their own writing read aloud to self-assess without embarrassment
- Learn how to pronounce words they don't hear in conversation
- Enjoy literature just for fun, developing a love of reading (Weitzman, 2022b)

Text-to-speech is a tool that benefits students with dyslexia, as the research in the next section shows. If you're looking for classroom ideas rather than research, feel free to skip the research section and dive straight into the subsequent section, Classroom Applications of Text-to-Speech (page 31).

How Text-to-Speech Helps Students With Dyslexia

In this section, we'll explore the research supporting the use of text-to-speech for students with dyslexia. Text-to-speech allows students to read and comprehend material at their intellectual level rather than their reading level. It can make the difference between failure and success in high school and beyond.

In the not-too-distant past, turning text into speech required a human reader, either in person or as a recording. With the advent of text-to-speech technology, students can have text read aloud anywhere at any time without feeling dependent on someone else. While high school teachers certainly can't read all their content aloud, they can give permission to use tech tools that do that. However it's accomplished, turning text into audio makes that text accessible to students with dyslexia.

The goal of using text-to-speech technology with students with dyslexia is to improve comprehension, so students can gain knowledge they would otherwise miss. Reading difficulty is compounded by lack of content knowledge when students can't access the text. Numerous research studies (Foxwell, 2023; Grusky, Taft, Naaman, & Azenkot, 2020; Keelor, Creaghead, Silbert, & Horowitz-Kraus, 2020; Salza & Alexander, 2019) provide evidence that students with dyslexia who use text-to-speech show improved comprehension compared to students with dyslexia who read without the aid of text-to-speech.

Although text-to-speech does not teach students to read, it does improve comprehension and vocabulary. If reading intervention in the early grades has failed to produce literacy, it's not time to give up. In a meta-study published in the *Journal of Learning Disabilities*, Sarah G. Wood, Jerad H. Moxley, Elizabeth L. Tighe, and Richard K. Wagner (2018) explain that intervention is the preferred approach in the early grades. Thus, elementary school efforts with struggling readers tend to center on teaching decoding skills.

If intervention fails to give the student sufficient reading skill to comprehend grade-level material by high school, Wood and colleagues (2018) conclude it's time to switch to compensation in the form of technology that reads for the student. After analyzing six studies that provided text-to-speech technology and charting the results compared to similar groups of students without this help, Wood and colleagues (2018) find that text-to-speech improves reading comprehension for individuals with reading disabilities.

In another study, professor of education Neeti Bhola (2022) studied a group of twenty students with dyslexia. The experimental group of ten students was taught with text-to-speech software, while the control group of ten students received no treatment. The two groups had the same average score on the pretest. The posttest four months later showed that the text-to-speech group had "significantly improved" scores while the control group remained the same (Bhola, 2022, p. 53). Bhola (2022) concludes that text-to-speech "contributed to remarkable gains in the achievement of students with dyslexia" (p. 51).

Colleges and universities also encourage students with dyslexia to use text-to-speech technology, so high school students can look forward to taking this tool with them into higher education. For example, Yale University's (n.d.) Student Accessibility Services offers the following tools.

- **Kurzweil 3000:** Kurzweil 3000 (www.kurzweil3000.com) allows users to hear text aloud. In addition to listening to text, users can highlight vital information, print notes, and create readable PDFs, mind maps, and even audio notes using the voice note tool.

- **NaturalReader:** NaturalReader (www.naturalreaders.com) is a web- and app-based text-to-speech reader for PDFs, Word documents, and various other electronic files. The benefit of this software is that the premium voices allow students to have a wider range of natural-sounding voices that work for them. In addition to using the app on a smartphone, users can also can install it as a browser plug-in.

- **Microsoft Edge:** This web browser comes with a built-in read-aloud function. Users can activate this function either by highlighting text and then right clicking the text to select "Read Aloud" or by clicking the open book button in the Edge address bar. This feature has an array of voices that can be adjusted for speed. Edge also reads PDFs.

- **Microsoft Word:** This word processor includes natural-sounding voices in its Dictate voice feature.

- **Apple Spoken Content:** A native feature found in Apple devices under the system preferences menu allows users to highlight and then press a shortcut key (option + esc for Macs, highlight and press *speak* on iPhones) to have the highlighted content read out loud. This feature offers limited voices but users can alter reading speeds.

- **Adobe Acrobat Reader:** This PDF viewer has an internal text-to-speech read-aloud feature accessible from the View tab in the menu bar. The downside of using the Adobe Acrobat Reader is that the documents are not always immediately accessible, and this software is not as robust in features. It does not allow for custom voices or speed adjustment when reading text aloud.

Suzie Glassman (2021), whose daughter is dyslexic, recommends in her article for *Wired* that students try a variety of text-to-speech tools to find the one that works best for them. Her picks include Voice Dream Reader (www.voicedream.com), Learning Ally (https://learningally.org), Bookshare (www.bookshare.org), Speechify (https://speechify.com), and digital scanning pens such as C-Pen ReaderPen (https://cpen.com/products/readerpen), Scanmarker Air (https://scanmarker.com), and Ectaco C-Pen (www.ectaco.com/cpen-30).

While much dyslexia research focuses on reading techniques or comprehension, some researchers seek to uncover ways to improve readers' receptivity. Educators report that students with dyslexia often appear to let their minds wander when reading (Eide & Eide, 2023). This tendency can also negatively impact comprehension.

Using Text-to-Speech Tools | 29

In response to this concern, research by Paola Bonifacci, Elisa Colombini, Michele Marzocchi, Valentina Tobia, and Lorenzo Desideri (2022) reveals that students with dyslexia are significantly more on task while using text-to-speech than while doing self-paced reading. Bonifacci and colleagues (2022) suggest that alleviating the cognitive load associated with decoding in students with dyslexia allows them to be more on task, or conversely, being involved in decoding increases the likelihood of mind wandering. They further state that "being free from the decoding load also increases their comprehension scores, although not sufficiently to reach typical readers' performance" (Bonifacci et al., 2022, p. 451).

Vocabulary also plays a key role in reading comprehension. As Kyle Redford (n.d.), the education editor at the Yale Center for Dyslexia & Creativity, points out:

> Standardized tests, humanities teachers, and the culture at large reward those with a strong vocabulary. On a subtle level, vocabulary is often used as an unconscious gauge to determine someone's level of intelligence. But much less subtly, having a strong working vocabulary helps one make meaning from the oral and written world. It should be no surprise that students with dyslexia struggle with written vocabulary. Often complex words are challenging because of difficult pronunciations. Students with dyslexia may even know the written word when used in a context or read aloud, but on a written word list it means nothing.

Redford (n.d.) recommends turning words into speech, either electronically or by a teacher reading aloud. He notes that hearing words in meaningful context improves vocabulary, which in turn increases comprehension. While reading aloud is great at any age, high school students need text-to-speech tools so that the reading their peers do is also accessible to them.

Dyslexia research is ongoing, and text-to-speech technology continues to evolve. Combining research and technology produces new and wonderful opportunities for high school students with dyslexia. Of course, as a high school teacher, you want your students to comprehend your subject. Reading has no value without comprehension. Merely decoding isn't the same as comprehending.

As *Education Week* (2023) states:

> Anyone who's ever scratched their head over their car manual or struggled to parse a website's terms of service knows: It's hard to read about a topic you don't really understand. It's a common-sense statement that's backed by research. Studies have shown that readers use their background knowledge—vocabulary, facts, and conceptual understanding—to comprehend the text they read. Much of this evidence isn't new. But it's received more attention now, amid the Science of Reading movement.

Since processing spoken language (narrative reasoning) is a strength for students with dyslexia (Eide & Eide, 2023), using text-to-speech tools to build background knowledge and vocabulary through listening allows students with dyslexia to fill in knowledge gaps that their reading peers may not have.

Complex sentences simply cannot be understood by slowly sounding out one word at a time. Thus, a dyslexic reader may decipher all the words but have no idea what the sentence means because the time it takes to decipher has exceeded working memory capacity. Students with dyslexia may compensate by reading each sentence multiple times until they have memorized it and can say it fast enough to understand the meaning.

Students with dyslexia often need to tackle each word anew, as though they've never seen it before, in order to decipher it. Without the automaticity that neurotypical readers enjoy, complex written material becomes inaccessible (Montgomery, Gillam, & Evans, 2021). Because of this, even students who have managed to learn phonics and sound out words may still be unable to comprehend high school–level reading. Additionally, the time this takes makes most assignments impossible.

No wonder high school students with dyslexia often reach a quitting point and give up. This is exactly the point where a teacher with tech tool knowledge can make all the difference. By offering the option of text-to-speech as an alternative to unsupported reading, the daunting task of reading becomes possible and hope can be restored.

Classroom Applications of Text-to-Speech

You can start changing the climate for students with dyslexia when you walk into your classroom tomorrow. To begin, introduce text-to-speech and inform your students that it's a tool they can use in every part of life: jobs, personal correspondence, and anywhere people want to listen to the printed word. Let your students know that text-to-speech use is welcome in your classroom and may be an important tool for supporting their efforts. Your most important role here is giving permission and time to find and use this technology.

It's helpful to give your students class time to access text-to-speech on their phones, computers, or tablets and then practice using it. This is time well spent. Students can quickly become frustrated if they can't make text-to-speech work at home. When you provide practice time in the classroom, you will be able to see who is struggling with the technology and assist them so text-to-speech becomes a seamless addition to your classroom.

Introducing text-to-speech as a classroom option won't take a lot of time. One class period is generally plenty. You can do so as part of another lesson. For example, if the class needs to cover some reading material, use that material to practice using these tools.

Furthermore, you don't need to know how to turn on text-to-speech on every device. Consider having the class group themselves by device: phone, computer, or tablet. Then subdivide by Android or iOS. It's likely that a student in each group will be able to guide the group to text-to-speech on their devices.

Another, even easier, route is to use your school's online environment, which almost certainly has text-to-speech available. Most high schools now use a schoolwide program to organize everything from grades to class schedules and calendars. It's where teachers can get attendance lists and students can check their grades. The most used platform is Google Classroom. There are many others including Blackboard Learn, Schoolology, EducateMe, Moodle, Schoox, and Brightspace. New platforms are coming out all the time, designed for various types of schools and settings.

On most of these platforms, including Google Classroom, a student can sign in, go to settings or preferences, and select the Accessibility option. Under Accessibility, select Text-to-Speech or Select-to-Speak. Once students have turned the function on, they can highlight any text they want to hear read aloud.

Some students may find text-to-speech such a game changer that they ask for more advanced apps than the school offers. There are many such apps, available on any app store. Our personal favorite is Voice Dream Reader (www.voicedream.com/reader), which won an Apple Design Award and is available for iOS or Mac. It also has a school version that is more affordable for schools. We like it because it highlights the line it's reading and it offers a variety of excellent voices. Also, students can speed up or slow down the voices for better comprehension. Another favorite app you might want to consider is Speechify (https://speechify.com).

While text-to-speech tools are often seen as accommodations, this is a holdover from a time when such tools were expensive for schools. That is no longer the case. This is a tool everyone can use to be more productive and avoid the slow-decoding learning barrier.

Teachers are often wary of accommodations in an educational setting because, even if necessary, they can take up valuable preparation and class time and may not address an actual student need. Accommodations such as preferential seating, extra test-taking time, and notetakers may take the place of needed interventions to raise skill level. These are reasonable concerns. However, text-to-speech should not be seen as merely an accommodation, but as a tool for all students to use as needed. That it allows students with dyslexia to participate fully in your classroom without labels or embarrassment is icing on the cake.

Psychology and education scholar Benjamin J. Lovett (2021) addresses concerns about accommodations:

> Research on current accommodation practices raises two distinct equity-related concerns. First, students from privileged backgrounds are more likely to receive certain accommodations even without adequate evidence of need; this can provide an unfair boost in performance and widen gaps among students. Second, when students from less privileged backgrounds are given accommodations, the incentive for schools to provide academic remediation, compensatory strategies, and coping skills is lessened, leaving these students in a worse position when accommodations are not available outside of educational settings. (p. 1)

Given that text-to-speech is widely available on phones and computers, it has become just one more learning tool that can benefit all students.

Access Text-to-Speech Tools

Of course, technologies are changing swiftly, so we won't even try to guess how to best access text-to-speech on every phone, computer, or tablet. By the time you read this, it would have changed. But you can easily find this information with some online searching or by asking colleagues.

Once you identify an app you want to use, we also recommend searching YouTube for instructional videos about using it effectively. For example, you could search for "How to enable text-to-speech in Google Docs." Each of your students may need to do it differently depending on which device they're using, but fortunately, your students are likely to be tech savvy and these tools are designed to be as easy to use as possible.

At a higher price point than text-to-speech apps, there are scanning pens, such as C-Pen and Scanmarker Pro, that a reader can roll over a word or sentence to have it read aloud. This option can be wonderful for students who are approaching independent reading but still need assistance with new vocabulary.

Invite Students to Share Their Technology Skills

It's important to keep in mind that you are not the only person who can assist students who are having difficulty with the technology. We've discovered that students who know they have dyslexia often gravitate to technology and have knowledge they can share with all students. They may experience an emotional boost as they help their classmates navigate new technology—a role they rarely find themselves in with their peers.

Over the next few weeks, you or a student can demonstrate using text-to-speech on any assignment. Ask students to show how they use text-to-speech to do their reading assignments while doing something else, such as exercising, working, or babysitting. This will open worlds of possibility for all students. It is a life changer for students with dyslexia.

Students can use in-class practice time to collaborate with each other and with you while they figure out how to enable text-to-speech as part of learning activities in your existing units. Even if some of that learning time goes to watching YouTube videos to help them gain the necessary text-to-speech skills, this time will pay off as students become more involved and successful—fewer behavior problems, less need to assist slow readers, and a more positive atmosphere in class.

Look for Audiobook Sources

When assigning book-length readings, investigate and ask for student input on the best audiobook sources. There may be multiple sources for audio versions of a book, including your school library or local library. Classics are often free—on LibriVox (https://librivox.org) or YouTube, for example. Reading quality varies, so experiment with those you identify or ask students to recommend the ones they like.

Audiobooks may be read by humans or by computers. Computer-generated voices used to be robotic and far less interesting than human readers. A great human reader is still the epitome of listening pleasure, but text-to-speech is now hard to distinguish from human speech and is improving every day.

Further, great readers in your class may realize there's a chance to use their skills by recording their own version of the book and uploading it to YouTube or another video hosting site, or distributing directly to you or their peers. Their classmates may love listening to someone they know reading the book. Students with dyslexia may suddenly learn they love literature.

Save Teacher Time Too

If you need to plow through large amounts of reading for a continuing education class or you'd love to be in a book club but just don't have the time, consider using this tool yourself. It allows you to read while doing other things such as driving or folding laundry. Kate Griggs, founder of MadeByDyslexia.org, says text-to-speech "allows you to proofread documents and read long text without fatigue" (Made by Dyslexia, n.d.). This applies to tired teachers as well as to students with dyslexia.

How to Address Pushback From Naysayers

Hopefully, you will have no need to defend your classroom choices to anyone—but if you do, here are a few common concerns you may hear from other educators or student caregivers.

"My textbook is paper, so who's going to read it aloud?"

In any classroom, especially mathematics and science, we encourage you to consider an electronic textbook that allows text-to-speech. Textbooks that include homework platforms that read problems or questions out loud can free students to do their best work. Inquire whether your school has an account with a digital textbook provider like Learning Ally (https://learningally.org), which also provides many other services for struggling readers. The reasonable fees are well worth it for a school. However, administrators may not realize that these services are valuable at the high school level.

"Audiobooks just make students lazy."

Actually, the opposite happens. Providing multiple ways for students to interact with the text can increase interest and participation for all students. Some students will find reading text more enjoyable, and some will prefer listening. By making it easy to choose and by not valuing one way over another, you are including more students and encouraging a more diverse classroom. When given this choice, students read more, not less. Listening to a book is not lazy—it's one great way to learn.

"I got through school without audiobooks, and so should they."

Forcing students to do things the way they were done in the past isn't realistic or helpful. Not all students read easily, so providing text-to-speech options validates the diversity of your students. Students who try for years to read but find it's still out of reach for them are likely to give up. You have the power to help them along a better path.

For added insight into the power of turning text into speech for students with dyslexia, you may find helpful Yvonna's interview with Fernette Eide, coauthor of *The Dyslexic Advantage* (Eide & Eide, 2023). This hour-long interview about why audio resources such as audiobooks and text-to-speech are so important for students with dyslexia is accessible on the Dyslexic Advantage YouTube channel (Dyslexic Advantage, 2023).

Summary

In this summary section, we offer a quick list of the main points covered in this chapter, followed by questions for reflection. We are also excited to share on page 40 Vicki's sample lesson plan for introducing text-to-speech in your classroom, which she developed over time and with much classroom experimentation. It's designed to make it easy to link text-to-speech instruction time to existing standards and IEP and 504 goals.

- Text-to-speech is software that turns printed text into audio. It's available free on both PC and Mac and on most smartphones.

- Research assures us that students with dyslexia using text-to-speech show improved comprehension.

- Text-to-speech can be integrated into any curriculum by giving students permission and time to try it.

- Using text-to-speech in your classroom will satisfy many of the IEP and 504 goals which you may be responsible to provide.

- Text-to-speech saves time for your struggling readers with dyslexia and can also save time for teachers by allowing them to do other tasks while listening to necessary readings.

Reflection

Use the following questions to further consider this chapter's new tool and how you can use it to help struggling readers.

1. How comfortable are you with text-to-speech? Have you used it before?

2. Can you think of students in your classroom who might be natural leaders in helping other students adopt text-to-speech?

3. Does your school have an online environment such as Google Classroom, and does it offer a text-to-speech option? What are your concerns or ideas about using it?

4. How might you ask students to use text-to-speech with their own writing and listen to themselves?

5. How might text-to-speech help those students who don't struggle as much with reading?

Reproducible Forms With Suggested Standards and IEP and 504 Goals

When you use one or two class periods to teach using text-to-speech, you meet multiple state standards, IEP goals, 504 accommodations, and various inclusion requirements. The reproducible "Sample Text-to-Speech Lesson Plan" (page 40) is an example of a text-to-speech lesson that Vicki used with excellent results in her high school classroom. We will use this lesson plan format for all the lesson plan examples in the book. There's a blank lesson plan template in the appendix (page 173) for your own use when lesson planning. You can also go to **go.SolutionTree.com/literacy** to download the blank reproducible version of the template.

The following lesson plan shows a classroom activity to instruct students in using a text-to-speech tool. This particular tool was currently available when this book was published at no cost to the teacher if the district used Google. If funding is available, we encourage you to research other text-to-speech tools that offer a more comprehensive approach, including the ability to slow down or speed up the reader. These would include apps such as Speechify and Dragon NaturallySpeaking.

Once the initial training is done, text-to-speech becomes an accepted part of the classroom culture. The accommodations and standards continue to be met throughout the semester, without any need to revisit the text-to-speech training. The form takes several pages because it allows you to simply check off how you are meeting various goals, rather than referring to the standards and accommodations repeatedly and writing them out yourself each time. The goal of this form is to save you time.

To clarify some terminology, *accommodations* are adjustments that allow a student to demonstrate knowledge, skills, and abilities without lowering learning or performance expectations and without changing what is being measured. *Modifications* change the nature of instruction and assessments and what students are expected to learn.

Numerous entities ask teachers to demonstrate how a lesson meets specific requirements such as WICOR (writing, inquiry, collaboration, organization, and reading), Bloom's taxonomy, special education accommodations and modifications, essential questions, and so on. Since school districts' lesson plan structures can be so different, we have included how the lesson could fulfill as many of these as possible. We encourage you to use what you can and leave the rest. Or, at the very least, our lesson plan will spark an idea for a classroom activity perfect for your students.

Sample Text-to-Speech Lesson Plan

Unit or Topic: Text-to-Speech

Days: One to two

Content Standards
List the standards applicable to this unit or topic:
Anchor standard, CCSS.ELA-Literacy.RI.11-12.1—Cite strong and thorough textual evidence to support analysis of what the text says explicitly as well as inferences drawn from the text, including determining where the text leaves matters uncertain.

Content Objectives: What are students learning? Students will learn how to use a text-to-speech tool to enable them to listen to text used in the assignment.	**Language Objectives:** How will students learn it? Students will install the Read Aloud function in Google Docs and practice using it by reading and listening to text provided by the teacher, then responding.
Essential Questions: How can a student access a text-to-speech tool and use it to analyze and draw inferences from a piece of text?	**Bloom's Taxonomy:** Check those that apply. The essential question is . . . ✓ Low (Knowledge and Comprehension) ✓ Middle (Application and Analysis) ✓ High (Synthesis and Evaluation) — Psychomotor (Physical Speed and Accuracy)

Building Background
Prior Knowledge: What do students need to know before the lesson?
Students need to know how to open a blank document in Google Docs on a computer using the Chrome browser. (Other internet browsers may not be able to access the Read Aloud extension.)
Key Vocabulary: text-to-speech, read aloud, extensions

Lesson Delivery

Instructional Time: Approximately fifty minutes

Lesson Sequence:

Install Read Aloud as an extension in Google Docs using a Google Chrome browser (adaptable for other word processing programs and browsers).

Note: Depending on the number of students in the room and proximity to each other, headphones may be a good option.

As versions of Chrome change over time, review the steps in number 2 and modify as needed.

1. Instruct students to open a Google Doc using the Chrome browser.
2. Instuct students to:
   a. Go to Extensions on toolbar
   b. Choose Add Ons, then Get Add Ons
   c. Search for "Read Aloud TTS"
   d. Install
   e. Choose their Google account
   f. Choose Continue
   g. Click on Allow
   h. Go to Extension on toolbar in Google Docs
   i. Click on Read Aloud
   j. Open the sidebar (this may take a few seconds as it loads the first time)
   k. Type a few test sentences into the document
   l. Highlight the text
   m. Click on arrow button in Read Aloud sidebar
3. Students may experiment with language, voice, speed, and pitch options in the sidebar.
4. Have students open the text you provided and "read" the text by using Read Aloud.
5. Ask students to open a blank Google Doc and type their response to the following question: *What point is the author trying to make? Show how the author is making this point.*
6. Have students listen to what they have written to "copyedit" it before emailing it to another student, who will then listen to the document.
7. Give students time to research other text-to-speech tools. Have students investigate a text-to-speech tool that may be available on their cell phones.

Closure:
1. As a class, discuss how to use this tool in other classes.
2. Discuss the advantages and disadvantages of using a text-to-speech tool.

Materials and Supplies:
- Access to Google Docs
- Headphones, if needed
- A content-specific text that students will analyze, citing at least one example from the text that supports their analysis, to address these prompts: What is the point the author is trying to make? Show how the author is making this point.

WICOR (Writing, Inquiry, Collaboration, Organization, and Reading) Strategies

Depending on the school district, the following instructional strategy responses may be required for a lesson plan. This section includes definitions and sample activities that a district may not provide but could be useful.

Check all that apply and then underline the activity in that category.

✔ **Writing** (<u>prewrite</u>, <u>draft</u>, <u>respond</u>, <u>revise</u>, <u>edit</u>, <u>final draft</u>, class and textbook notes, learning logs)

__ **Inquiry** (Costa's levels of questions, skilled questioning, Socratic seminars, quick writes and discussion, critical thinking activities, writing questions, open-mindedness activities)

✔ **Collaboration** (group projects, study groups, jigsaw activities, response-edit-revision activities, <u>collaborative activities</u>)

__ **Organization** (tools, such as binders, calendars, planners, agendas, graphic organizers, and methods such as focused note-taking system, tutorials, study groups, project planning)

✔ **Reading** (SQ3R method [survey, question, <u>read</u>, recite, <u>review</u>], KWL charts [what I know, what I want to learn, what I learned], reciprocal teaching, think-alouds, reader response, graphic organizers, vocabulary building)

Strategies		
Check any or all that apply.		
Scaffolding: — Modeling — Guided Practice ✓ Independent Practice	**Describe here if needed:**	**Concept Development:** ✓ Similarities and Differences — Summarizing and Note-Taking — Reinforcing Effort and Providing Recognition — Nonlinguistic Representation — Generating and Testing Hypotheses
Practice and Application: ✓ Listening ✓ Reading ✓ Worksheet ✓ Writing ✓ Discussion — Hands-On or Manipulatives		
Interaction: ✓ Whole Class — Small Group — Partners ✓ Independent	**5E Lesson Planning:** — Engage (capture interest) ✓ Explore (experiment, simulate, or collaborate) — Explain (discuss and define concepts) — Elaborate (apply new knowledge) ✓ Evaluate (assess to gauge comprehension)	**Engaging Qualities:** ✓ Personal Response — Clear and Modeled Expectations — Emotional and Intellectual Safety — Learning With Others — Sense of Audience ✓ Choice ✓ Novelty and Variety — Authenticity

page 4 of 7

Never Too Late © 2025 Solution Tree Press • SolutionTree.com
Visit **go.SolutionTree.com/literacy** to download this free reproducible.

Special Education Requirements

Accommodations—How to Instruct
(to make education more accessible for students with disabilities)

Examples: Timing and scheduling for classwork and tests; reduced-distraction setting; special equipment; presentation in large print; recorded or human-read books; responses using a scribe, graphic organizer, calculator, or speech-to-text equipment

Modifications—What to Instruct
(only for students with an IEP)

Examples: Use fewer concepts, ask different test questions, reduce number of problems, revise assignments, give hints or clues, modify tests, grade on effort, use alternative text and assignments, modify questions, shorten assignments, give open-book tests

Consider each of the following instructional areas. Where appropriate, describe the activity and check whether it was an accommodation or modification.

Instructional Area	Activity	Accommodation	Modification
Content			
Materials	Students will be trained on Read Aloud software.	✔	
Delivery			
Activity	Students will be given the option to use Read Aloud with their reading assignments.		✔

Never Too Late © 2025 Solution Tree Press • SolutionTree.com
Visit **go.SolutionTree.com/literacy** to download this free reproducible.

Review and Assessment

Consider the following questions before choosing the assessment:
- How will students receive feedback?
- How do students know what is expected of them?

Check all that apply and provide a brief description.

✓ Formative assessment (*for* learning; informal)

Examples: Identifying where students are and what their needs are, applying questioning strategies, using exit tickets, checking in with students

Identify where students are before the lesson by sending them an informal Google survey that asks if they know what text-to-speech is, which tools they may already use, and how they may currently be using the tool

__ **Summative assessment** (*of* learning; formal)

Examples: Grading, tests, quizzes, performance tasks, rubrics

Reflection

What do you need to change to facilitate improvement?

What will you do differently if students have not demonstrated mastery of the objective?

What would you add?

Specific things to consider on this text-to-speech lesson:

Check the teacher's attitude: Is the teacher's attitude one of enthusiasm and support when presenting the tool? This is a powerful tool that can change the life of a student with dyslexia and should be seen that way.

Reflect on time provided:
Did students have enough time to practice using the tool? Why or why not?

Source: AVID. (n.d.). WICOR (writing, inquiry, collaboration, organization, and reading). *Accessed at https://avidopenaccess.org/wp-content/uploads/2021/08/AVID-WICOR-flyer-080521_proofed.pdf on July 24, 2024;* Echevarría, J., Vogt, M., Short, D. J., & Toppel, K. (2024). Making content comprehensible for multilingual learners: The SIOP model (6th ed.). *Pearson;* Gerges, E. (2022, March 4). How to use the 5E model in your science classroom. *Edutopia. Accessed at www.edutopia.org/article/how-use-5e-model-your-science-classroom on April 9, 2024;* Idaho Special Education Support & Technical Assistance (SESTA). (2022). Idaho IEP guidance handbook: High-quality practices. *Accessed at https://idahotc.com/Portals/0/Resources/1007/The-Idaho-IEP-Guidance-Handbook.pdf on April 9, 2024;* National Governors Association Center for Best Practices & Council of Chief State School Officers. (2010). Common Core State Standards for English language arts and literacy in history/social studies, science, and technical subjects. *Authors. Accessed at https://corestandards.org/wp-content/uploads/2023/09/ELA_Standards1.pdf on January 5, 2025.*

CHAPTER 2

Using Speech-to-Text Tools

My spelling makes people laugh, but I was lucky to have a teacher who focused on what I was writing, not how I was spelling it. That let me explore my creativity.
—KEIRA KNIGHTLEY

Introducing speech-to-text as a dyslexia tool may prompt the question, "Why would a student with dyslexia need to turn speech into text? I thought reading, not writing, was the problem." This is a common misconception about dyslexia. However, the same neural differences that underlie the reading challenges of dyslexia also cause significant difficulty in putting words on paper.

Speech-to-text is the tool that can help students past this roadblock because it allows people to speak to a computer and have the computer type what they said, thus bypassing most of the difficulties with spelling, handwriting, and even typing.

Eide and Eide (2023) note, "Many individuals with dyslexia enjoy creative writing, even though they may have difficulty with formal academic writing or reading; so teachers should look carefully for signs of narrative ability . . . and use appropriate tutoring and accommodations" (p. 212).

In this chapter, we'll introduce speech-to-text as a tool that can free students with dyslexia to produce their best written work using their narrative strengths.

Some teachers may know all too well what it's like to struggle with writing due to dyslexia. For example, Ms. Januski, an educator in Arizona, is candid about her own difficulty spelling:

> One of my struggles has become a superpower . . . pause for dramatic effect . . . I can't spell. I don't mean I struggle a bit with spelling. I mean nearly every word. I try to memorize, or come up with a synonym that I can spell. Fun fact—I can spell synonym! (A. Januski, personal communication, May 24, 2023)

How Ms. Januski deals with her spelling challenge in the classroom is interesting. She tells us the following:

> One of the biggest and most humbling techniques that I use in my classroom is my Apple Watch. It sounds silly, but I'm no longer ashamed to ask my watch how to spell something. I used to think it was an unfair crutch, but I realized that I am teaching my students by example how to find information. (A. Januski, personal communication, May 24, 2023)

Ms. Januski is using one form of speech-to-text when she asks her watch to spell a word.

Speech-to-text technology goes far beyond getting your Apple Watch to spell words. In this chapter, we'll explore multiple ways to use speech-to-text to support students with dyslexia as they find their voices. We'll show that speech-to-text can be the tool that reveals unsuspected talent and frees students to produce work that truly reflects their abilities.

What Speech-to-Text Is

Speech-to-text, *voice-to-text*, *voice typing*, or *dictation technology* all refer to speech recognition software that converts the spoken word to typed text.

Speech-to-text applications use a computer-based microphone to pick up spoken words and turn them into printed text. Since microphones are integral to phones, modern computers, and many tablets, this tech tool is now widely available. It can be used to take notes about ideas while taking a walk or write papers for a class that would otherwise be dreaded. Indeed, many authors compose entire books using speech-to-text.

Of course, the computer program seldom writes exactly what the speaker intended—it writes what it "heard." This becomes a wonderful teaching opportunity, as we'll explain in the classroom section.

Although many companies charge for speech-to-text technology, Google, Apple, and others provide free versions and are upgradable to add more features for a modest fee. The company Nuance makes Dragon (https://nuance.com/dragon), paid software that provides robust speech-to-text technology that adapts more readily to regional accents and speech impediments. Nuance also offers versions that enunciate specific vocabulary better, such as medical, legal, and technical terminology.

A growing number of apps make speech-to-text available in a variety of ways for phones, computers, and tablets. Many schools use Google Classroom as their online environment. It has voice typing capability, so your students may already have easy access to excellent speech-to-text technology. The reproducible "Sample Speech-to-Text Lesson Plan" included at the end of this chapter (page 64) shows how to access Voice Typing using a classroom activity.

The research in the next section illustrates how speech-to-text technology can help students with dyslexia in the classroom. If you're looking for classroom ideas rather than research, feel free to skip the research section and dive straight into the subsequent section, Classroom Applications of Speech-to-Text (page 55).

How Speech-to-Text Helps Students With Dyslexia

As noted above, dyslexia affects students' ability to write as well as read. In fact, many students with dyslexia also deal with dysgraphia. *Dysgraphia* is a neurological difference that causes difficulty with handwriting and spelling (International Dyslexia Association, 2020b).

Because of this, students with dyslexia may be highly skilled in verbal language but find putting words on paper nearly impossible. As Eide and Eide (2020) state:

> [Gifted students] are often especially hard for parents and teachers to understand because they may have verbal IQs in the highly or profoundly gifted range and show every sign of verbal precocity. Yet, these same children might be unable to write the alphabet—even as teenagers.

Furthermore, if the student speaks well, the disappointing quality of their written work may make them avoid it altogether. This can give the impression that they are lazy. However, they might prefer to fail the class rather than embarrass themselves with work they consider inferior.

Speech-to-text allows students with dyslexia to get their great ideas down on paper by removing a roadblock and making it possible to produce written work that represents their true abilities. In this way, technology that assists with writing can help students with dyslexia.

Speech-to-text technology on computers and phones has been widely available in personal computing since the early 2000s (Strait, 2023). This has spurred an increasing number of research studies into how this tool affects writing output for students with dyslexia. Studies that collate and compare multiple studies can provide excellent insights for educators.

For example, researchers with the National Center on Educational Outcomes (NCEO) Linda Goldstone, Sheryl Lazarus, Rachel Olson, Andrew R. Hinkle, and Virginia A. Ressa (2021) compared results of six studies on the effects of using speech-to-text in education. They find that all six studies agree that speech-to-text results in better student writing.

Goldstone and her colleagues (2021) at the NCEO conclude the following:

> Overall, students [using speech-to-text] produced longer written text with fewer errors. However, speech-to-text is more effective for improving writing quality for secondary students compared to elementary students because they do more in-depth writing using more complex sentences, advanced vocabulary, and greater narrative development.

Since writing and spelling challenges are major barriers to success for students with dyslexia, these findings are significant for high school teachers.

Stanford University's School of Education researchers Sarah Levine, Hsiaolin Hsieh, Emily Southerton, and Rebecca Silverman (2023) investigated the use of speech-to-text in general education high school classrooms. The study invited 120 students to use speech-to-text as much or as little as they wanted during one school year. The researchers analyzed field notes, interviews, surveys, and student writing composed with and without speech-to-text supports (Levine et al., 2023).

Levine and colleagues (2023) find that students wrote more when they used speech-to-text than when they didn't. Over half of students found that speech-to-text eased the cognitive load of composition. Less than half of the students found that the tool constrained their composition. Some were put off by technical problems or embarrassment about speaking out loud in class. Students' choices to use speech-to-text correlated with special education designation but not other designations. Teachers were consistently positive about speech-to-text and planned to use it in future classes (Levine et al., 2023).

Note that in this study, all students were invited to use speech-to-text with no distinction made between those with a dyslexia diagnosis and those without. As discussed, we can expect 20 percent of students to exhibit symptoms of dyslexia (Yale Center for Dyslexia & Creativity, n.d.b). Therefore, the group of students in the Stanford study would have theoretically had around twenty-four students with dyslexia. However, over sixty students reported that speech-to-text made writing easier.

Levine and colleagues' (2023) findings align with our observations in the classroom. The important takeaway from this research is that speech-to-text proved to be a valuable tool for improving writing for over half of the students in the study, especially those with dyslexia. Furthermore, the study shows that speech-to-text is a viable option in high school classes allowing those who need it to try it without being singled out.

Because high school students with dyslexia often avoid turning in work that fails to meet their own standards, providing speech-to-text can change a student's class participation dramatically. Education scholars Marianne Engen Matre and David Lansing Cameron (2024) provide insight into how speech-to-text improves students' quality of writing, thus opening the door for them to feel comfortable handing in their work.

In a study of research on the use of speech-to-text in high school classrooms from 2000 to 2022, Matre and Carmeron (2024) conclude, "Results suggest that speech-to-text may increase pupils' abilities to produce texts with fewer errors, provide help with spelling and improve reading comprehension and word recognition" (p. 1). Such results make speech-to-text an important tool for any high school teacher.

Classroom Applications of Speech-to-Text

Your students may already be using speech-to-text on social media by sending voice texts. However, your job is to help them use speech-to-text to do their schoolwork and, by extension, any writing task. For every student who says they "know this already," there is another student who would benefit from using it but feels embarrassed to try.

To introduce speech-to-text into your classroom, discuss how it helps people work faster and smarter in their jobs. This is what the know-it-already student may be missing. It's a tool their future coworkers will likely use and you want them to feel comfortable with this technology. Express your hope that they will try it for at least one assignment in your class. Ask students to let you know what works for them and what doesn't so you can fine-tune your use of this technology.

It's important that all students learn and practice using speech-to-text. It must not be seen as an accommodation for a disability. While it's especially helpful for students with dyslexia, all students can benefit. After everyone is comfortable, students can opt to use it or not, depending on their preferences.

Spelling can be a huge hurdle for students with dyslexia. They realize their poor spelling makes their work come across as rushed and incompetent. Speech-to-text can help resolve spelling problems. Writers no longer have to self-generate their spelling. Instead, they focus on clearly pronouncing the word so the computer can type it for them. Of course, homophones are a challenge for most speech-to-text programs, but an online dictionary while proofreading helps.

For example, the student may clearly speak the sentence, "I prayed for my grandmother every day." The computer may type, "I preyed for my grandmother every day." By highlighting and looking up the word *preyed*, the student may be able to self-correct. However, no one catches all their own errors, so peer and teacher editing will never go out of style. Let students know this is just one reason why professional writers always employ editors.

After writing with the aid of speech-to-text, students still have to do the normal spell check and editing, of course. They may need to ask for assistance with this from a friend or family member. Because they've saved so much time by using speech-to-text and can produce a readable paper, they are more likely to make that effort. From the teacher's standpoint, helping a student edit becomes easier when what the student wants to say is already on the page.

Focus and sustained attention to task are common problems for students with dyslexia (Eide & Eide, 2023). Speech-to-text allows students to invest mental energy in the organization and content of their writing instead of focusing all mental power on typing or handwriting. Since speech-to-text speeds up this process dramatically, it allows the student to focus on the more complex and interesting aspects of writing. Motivation to write naturally follows when the student is pleased with their own work and can do it in a reasonable amount of time. By speeding up the writing process, maintaining focus and attention becomes easier and more rewarding. The following sections further explore ways to use speech-to-text in your classroom.

Create a Speech-to-Text–Friendly Classroom

To create a classroom that encourages the use of speech-to-text, arrange for a place where students can talk quietly to their computer or phone while voice typing. This may be difficult in your school setting, so brainstorm with students to explore the possibilities.

Yvonna used a large cardboard box from a refrigerator to craft a sound-dampening "office" for students who chose to use it for speech-to-text tasks. Some of your students may be eager to show their construction skills and amaze you with their creativity.

Speech-to-text works for any writing assignment. Ask students to outline ideas in their heads or on paper before starting to talk to the computer. This is good practice for all writing tasks.

Try Small-Group Editing

Editing is an important part of every writing assignment, whether using speech-to-text or not, and there are ways of making the process more accessible for students with dyslexia. One way to make editing both effective and more engaging is to have students work in small groups to edit their papers.

Students may be comfortable working in small groups to find errors stemming both from a student's dictation and from a speech-to-text translation of that dictation. This approach works well and aids in team building. The teacher plays an important role here by modeling how to find and correct errors while noticing and commenting on the great ideas or solid research students have done.

Few students know how to edit without specific guidance and examples. A checklist of things to look for can help student groups know how to proceed. Figure 2.1 (page 58) is a checklist for students to use when group editing speech-to-text papers prior to turning them in.

If students seem uncomfortable in their editing small groups, brainstorm with them about what would feel better. The groups may not have the right balance of strengths and talents. There could be personality clashes. Since groups are editing rather than grading, ensure students feel free to ask for help when needed. Students should always understand that the writing process is messy, which is why revision is such a vital part of it. Mistakes, whether speech-to-text generated or not, are to be expected.

- Are there ideas that the author could express better or in fewer words?
- Do subjects and verbs agree?
- Do pronouns and their antecedents agree in number and gender?
- Homophones such as *there*, *they're*, and *their* are commonly misused. Use a dictionary to check for correct usage, if needed.
- Do you see irritating repetition of two or more sentences starting the same way?
- Did the author use transition words (*first*, *second*, *next*, *however*, *thus*) where needed?
- Did the computer reproduce what the author intended?
- Correct any spelling errors. Using a spell checker is fine but watch out for those pesky homophones.
- Are all sources properly cited?

Figure 2.1: Speech-to-text editing checklist.

*Visit **go.solutiontree.com/literacy** to access a free reproducible version of this figure.*

It's important to keep editing upbeat and positive. Encouraging students to say what they like or find interesting in each other's papers builds a sense of safety. Some of the best learning happens when students detect mistakes that they can all playfully laugh at.

Small-group editing time is a great opportunity to introduce the Grammarly app. A free version of Grammarly is available (https://grammarly.com), which can make editing much more independent and fun for students, and which they will certainly find useful in high school, college, and beyond. Grammarly cleans up text by finding grammatical mistakes, spelling errors, and typos, and by suggesting corrections.

Save Teacher Time Too

High school students will benefit from using speech-to-text—but what about teachers? Teachers who are inundated with demands for documentation and reports can use voice typing to lighten the load. Simon Baddeley (2019), a teacher and blogger, writes:

> Using Voice Typing, it is possible to dictate a whole class set of individual and highly personalized comments in under an hour. You don't have to compromise on the quality of your comment in order to get the reports completed in a timely manner.

Access speech-to-text in Google Docs or Microsoft Word and play around with it. You will be pleasantly surprised. Check out the various settings. It will be easier to see what types of assignments to give students as you wander through the possible options.

No matter what subject you teach, there are times when students need to write. And there are times when you have to produce written documents. Offering your students and yourself the alternative of speech-to-text takes the pressure off. It may let you see hidden genius you didn't even suspect. It may also make it easier to improve your own overloaded workday.

How to Address Pushback From Naysayers

Hopefully, you will have no need to defend your classroom choices to anyone—but if you do, here are a few common concerns you may hear from other educators or student caregivers.

"I don't want students talking in my classroom, especially to a machine!"

It's true that a large class using speech-to-text can get too noisy for anyone to work productively. Allowing students to use headphones or earbuds will help cut down on the noise distraction. But it may still be too much, especially for students who are auditorily sensitive.

If there's no good place in your classroom for students to do this kind of work, it may be necessary to have them plan their outlines in class, then do their voice typing outside of school. It's not perfect, but it still provides a way for students with dyslexia to produce quality work. If you are extremely lucky, your school library has sound-proof study rooms that are perfect for voice typing.

"How are students supposed to learn to write if all they do is talk?"

That's the beauty of speech-to-text. It is the perfect bridge between verbal skills and writing. By seeing their own words on screen or printed out on paper and then editing those sentences and paragraphs with help, students actually learn to write in their own voice. It's powerful teaching, and the act of voicing their thoughts, then editing, and finally reading their own words imprints correct sentence structure, punctuation, spelling, paragraph structure, and much more. It sure beats struggling alone, hating the result, and then giving up.

"I'm old fashioned. I want students to hand in real paper that I can grade with a red pen."

Voice-typed documents can be marked or edited on Google Docs if you are comfortable with that, or the students can print out their papers and hand them in. Likewise, if you mark up actual papers, students can use these to edit their Google document and reprint it. It might be seen as a waste of paper, but for some, seeing the words on real paper is absolutely worth it.

"Some students don't speak clearly enough for the computer to understand them."

This is true. If a speech impediment or accent makes voice typing too difficult, that student will be better served by getting access to more feature-rich software, like Dragon NaturallySpeaking. This program is specifically designed to adjust itself to speech impediments and regional accents. Check for educational pricing. Your district may already have a subscription, so you may just need to ask the right people to get access to it. Talk to the special education educators and administrators in your building. Call special education at the district office. It's possible there is funding to help your school get the software.

Students whose speech impediment prevents using speech-to-text may also benefit from an individually paced touch-typing class, which may be available through the special education department. Making this happen isn't your responsibility as a high school teacher, but a quick word to a student or special educator may open doors that neither knew existed. One possible advantage of speech-to-text for a student who struggles with speaking is that voice typing will soon help them hear how they sound to others, and it may encourage them to self-correct.

"If students can make As in my class without speech-to-text, why should I bother with it?"

Even the most literate students will benefit from exposure to speech-to-text, as it's a tool their future coworkers or family members may use, even if they don't. It's also a fun change of pace from writing papers the traditional way. However, you can assure your students that once they have tried speech-to-text, they are free to respond to assignments in the way that works best for them.

Summary

In this summary section, we offer a quick list of the main points covered in this chapter, followed by questions for reflection. We also share on page 64 Vicki's sample lesson plan for introducing speech-to-text in your classroom, which she developed over time and with much classroom experimentation. It's designed to make it easy to link speech-to-text instruction time to existing standards and IEP and 504 goals.

- Speech-to-text, also known as voice typing, is speech-recognition computer software that converts the spoken word to typed text.

- Research shows that students with dyslexia who use speech-to-text write more extensively and use higher-level writing skills than those who do not have access.

- Introducing speech-to-text into a high school classroom removes dyslexic roadblocks to success such as writing or typing so slowly that students lose focus and inability to spell words correctly.

- While speech-to-text can be noisy if used in a classroom, and some students will prefer traditional typing, the benefit of speech-to-text for students with dyslexia is well worth a class session or two of training. Any student who struggles with writing may find speech-to-text sets them free to create with the written word.

- Speech-to-text allows you to easily fulfill many state standards, IEP goals, and 504 requirements for students who have them. Using the lesson template provided, you can quickly check off the standards and goals that apply.

- Even if you are a superb speller and a lightning-fast typist, you may find that speech-to-text allows you to fulfill the paperwork requirements of your school more easily. Anything that reduces the paperwork load for teachers is a good thing.

Reflection

Use the following questions to further consider this chapter's new tool and how you can use it to help struggling readers.

1. Have you used speech-to-text yourself? If so, what has been your experience? If not, is it a tool you would like to try?

2. How do you think your students might react to the speech-to-text tool?

3. What might you learn about yourself and your students as you use speech-to-text in the classroom?

4. What difficulties do you think you might encounter as you introduce speech-to-text into your classroom? What might you do to avoid these difficulties?

5. Which of your students might you imagine particularly enjoying or benefiting from speech-to-text? Why?

Reproducible Forms With Suggested Standards and IEP and 504 Goals

As we did for text-to-speech in chapter 1, here we offer a "Sample Speech-to-Text Lesson Plan" (page 64) for teaching speech-to-text in your classroom. Text-to-speech and speech-to-text tools can be used separately or in tandem, but we've had better results teaching them as separate tools. Once the students know how to use both tools, they will naturally combine them when needed. When you're ready to create your own lesson plans, visit **go.SolutionTree.com/literacy** to access the blank lesson plan template.

Sample Speech-to-Text Lesson Plan

Unit or Topic: Speech-to-Text

Days: One

Content Standards
List the standards applicable to this unit or topic:
Anchor standard, CCSS.ELA-Literacy.W.11–12.6—Use technology, including the internet, to produce, publish, and update individual or shared writing products in response to ongoing feedback, including new arguments or information.

Content Objectives:	Language Objectives:
What are students learning?	How will students learn it?
They're learning how to use a speech-to-text tool to verbally record information into a document in a fast and accurate manner.	Students will be introduced to the speech-to-text tool Voice Typing in Google Docs.
Essential Questions:	**Bloom's Taxonomy:**
How does the student use Voice Typing in Google Docs to write text?	Check those that apply.
How can the tool support the ability of a student with dyslexia to produce written work?	The essential question is . . .
	✓ Low (Knowledge and Comprehension)
	✓ Middle (Application and Analysis)
	✓ High (Synthesis and Evaluation)
	___ Psychomotor (Physical Speed and Accuracy)

Building Background
Prior Knowledge: What do students need to know before the lesson?
Students need to know how to open a blank Google Doc using the Chrome browser. Students need to have experience completing an activity in class and providing a short response, such as an observation of a science lab or a response to a literary reading.
Key Vocabulary: speech-to-text, voice typing

Lesson Delivery

Instructional Time: Approximately fifty minutes

Lesson Sequence:

Learn to use Voice Typing in Google Docs using a Google Chrome browser (adaptable for other word processing programs and browsers).

Note: Depending on the number of students in the room and proximity to each other, headphones may be a good option.

As versions of Chrome change over time, review the steps in number 2 and modify as needed.

1. Instruct students to use the Chrome browser and open a Google Doc.
2. Instruct students to:
   a. Go to Tools
   b. Choose Voice Typing
   c. Click on the microphone and start talking
   d. See how their words will come up as written text on the screen
3. Point out that punctuation marks such as *period* and *exclamation point* are spoken.
4. Have students experiment for a few minutes on their own using Voice Typing. Have them experiment with different punctuation marks.
5. Provide a content-specific piece of writing (a couple of short paragraphs) that students can record into the document. For example, have them access their textbook and record some paragraphs of their choosing.
6. Have students open a new blank document.
7. Refer to the class assignment that students would normally type or write. Instead of manually typing or handwriting the assignment, have them use Voice Typing and hand it in.

Bonus fun activity!

Have students explore the translation option, going to Tools, and then Translate.

Note: Voice Typing may not work in other languages. Documents may need to be translated back into English for Voice Typing to show up on the drop-down menu under tools.

Closure:

1. As a class, discuss how to use this tool in other classes.
2. Discuss the advantages and disadvantages of using a speech-to-text tool.

Materials and Supplies:
- Access to Google Docs
- Headphones, if needed
- A short text in the content area that students can practice reading into the document using Voice Typing

WICOR (Writing, Inquiry, Collaboration, Organization, and Reading) Strategies

Depending on the school district, the following instructional strategy responses may be required for a lesson plan. This section includes definitions and sample activities that a district may not provide but could be useful.

Check all that apply and then underline the activity in that category.

- ✓ **Writing** (<u>prewrite</u>, <u>draft</u>, <u>respond</u>, revise, edit, final draft, <u>class and textbook notes</u>, learning logs)
- __ **Inquiry** (Costa's levels of questions, skilled questioning, Socratic seminars, quick writes and discussion, critical thinking activities, writing questions, open-mindedness activities)
- __ **Collaboration** (group projects, study groups, jigsaw activities, response-edit-revision activities, collaborative activities)
- __ **Organization** (tools such as binders, calendars, planners, agendas, graphic organizers, and methods such as focused note-taking system, tutorials, study groups, project planning)
- __ **Reading** (SQ3R method [survey, question, read, recite, review], KWL charts [what I know, what I want to learn, what I learned], reciprocal teaching, think-alouds, reader response, graphic organizers, vocabulary building)

Strategies		
Check any or all that apply.		
Scaffolding: — Modeling — Guided Practice ✓ Independent Practice	**Describe here if needed:**	**Concept Development:** ✓ Similarities and Differences — Summarizing and Note-Taking — Reinforcing Effort and Providing Recognition — Nonlinguistic Representation — Generating and Testing Hypotheses
Practice and Application: — Listening ✓ Reading — Worksheet ✓ Writing ✓ Discussion — Hands-On or Manipulatives		
Interaction: ✓ Whole Class — Small Group — Partners ✓ Independent	**5E Lesson Planning:** — Engage (capture interest) ✓ Explore (experiment, simulate, or collaborate) — Explain (discuss and define concepts) — Elaborate (apply new knowledge) ✓ Evaluate (assess to gauge comprehension)	**Engaging Qualities:** ✓ Personal Response — Clear and Modeled Expectations — Emotional and Intellectual Safety — Learning With Others — Sense of Audience ✓ Choice ✓ Novelty and Variety — Authenticity

Special Education Requirements

Accommodations—How to Instruct
(to make education more accessible for students with disabilities)

Examples: Timing and scheduling for classwork and tests; reduced-distraction setting; special equipment; presentation in large print; recorded or human-read books; responses using a scribe, graphic organizer, calculator, or speech-to-text equipment

Modifications—What to Instruct
(only for students with an IEP)

Examples: Use fewer concepts, ask different test questions, reduce number of problems, revise assignments, give hints or clues, modify tests, grade on effort, use alternative text and assignments, modify questions, shorten assignments, give open-book tests

Consider each of the following instructional areas. Where appropriate, describe the activity and check whether it was an accommodation or modification.

Instructional Area	Activity	Accommodation	Modification
Content	Students will be trained on how to use voice typing.	✔	
Materials	Students will use voice typing software.	✔	
Delivery			
Activity	Students will be given the option to use voice typing with their reading assignments.		✔

Review and Assessment
Consider the following questions before choosing the assessment: • How will students receive feedback? • How do students know what is expected of them?
Check all that apply and provide a brief description. ✓ **Formative assessment** (*for* learning; informal) Examples: Identifying where students are and what their needs are, applying questioning strategies, using exit tickets, checking in with students Identify where students are before the lesson by sending them an informal Google survey that asks if they know what speech-to-text is, which tools they may already use, and how they may currently be using the tool ___ **Summative assessment** (*of* learning; formal) Examples: Grading, tests, quizzes, performance tasks, rubrics

Reflection
What do you need to change to facilitate improvement?
What will you do differently if students have not demonstrated mastery of the objective?

What would you add?

Specific things to consider on this speech-to-text lesson:

Check the teacher's attitude: Is the teacher's attitude one of enthusiasm and support when presenting the tool? This is a powerful tool that can change the life of a student with dyslexia and should be seen that way.

Reflect on time provided:

Did students have enough time to practice using the tool? Why or why not?

Source: AVID. (n.d.). WICOR (writing, inquiry, collaboration, organization, and reading). Accessed at https:// avidopenaccess.org/wp-content/uploads/2021/08/AVID-WICOR-flyer-080521_proofed.pdf on July 24, 2024; Echevarría, J., Vogt, M., Short, D. J., & Toppel, K. (2024). Making content comprehensible for multilingual learners: The SIOP model (6th ed.). *Pearson; Gerges, E. (2022, March 4). How to use the 5E model in your science classroom.* Edutopia. *Accessed at www.edutopia.org/article/how-use-5e-model-your-science-classroom on April 9, 2024; Idaho Special Education Support & Technical Assistance (SESTA). (2022).* Idaho IEP guidance handbook: High-quality practices. *Accessed at https://idahotc.com/Portals/0/Resources/1007/The-Idaho-IEP -Guidance-Handbook.pdf on April 9, 2024; National Governors Association Center for Best Practices & Council of Chief State School Officers. (2010).* Common Core State Standards for English language arts and literacy in history/social studies, science, and technical subjects. *Authors. Accessed at https://corestandards.org/wp-content /uploads/2023/09/ELA_Standards1.pdf on January 5, 2025.*

CHAPTER 3

Tracking With Audio-Assisted Reading

*Seeing words along with hearing them
helped me remember what the words looked like.
Sounding words out never seemed to work.*
—TONY FISHEL

Tony Fishel grew up in a close, attentive family. His mom, Judy, was a mathematics and science educator in a variety of schools. Tony enjoyed a culturally rich childhood, growing up in the Philippines and the Marshall Islands. Tony had the advantage of Judy's constant help, good teachers, and three and a half years of tutoring for dyslexia. However, he still couldn't read. He managed school only by having Judy read everything to him.

Thanks to a suggestion by his middle school special education teacher, Tony discovered audiobooks from the library for the blind. Text-to-speech didn't exist yet. He got audio recordings of *The Lord of the Rings* trilogy by J. R. R. Tolkien. Then, he asked his parents for printed copies of the books.

When he had both, he began listening to the audiobooks while tracking along visually with the reader. He read each book in the trilogy four times, first tracking along with the tape and then struggling alone. To his surprise, this effort finally helped him achieve the reading level he desired.

Tony met daunting challenges and difficulties that would cause many to give up. But he persevered, earning not only a bachelor's degree in physics but also a master's degree in education. He's currently a high school physics teacher.

Tony and Judy Fishel cowrote a book, *How Tony Learned to Read: Growing Up Dyslexic* (Fishel & Fishel, 2021). After reading it, Yvonna spoke with Judy Fishel and then interviewed Tony about his experience. A recording of the interview is available on YouTube (Graham, 2022).

The instructional method that Tony Fishel discovered on his own is called *tracking*. It means looking at printed text while simultaneously listening to the same text. Yvonna told her students that the words would go in through their ears and their eyes at the same time and get locked together in their brains. That's a simplified picture of what happens neurologically, and it's our most powerful tech tool.

In chapter 1 (page 23), we explored text-to-speech tools that let students who can't read high school–level text access the same information as their peers. Chapter 2 (page 49) introduced speech-to-text, which allows students with dyslexia to write at their verbal level, unhampered by handwriting, typing, and spelling difficulties.

In this chapter, we focus on tracking, a profoundly effective method of combining written text with spoken text. This technique is so simple it's often overlooked. In our own teaching, we began observing the effects of tracking in a purposeful and systematic way in a high school classroom. Surprisingly, we found that students with and without dyslexia responded positively, and classroom engagement improved.

Vicki's high school classroom became our testing lab to find tools that would assist students with dyslexia without disrupting or slowing classroom instruction.

What Tracking Is

Tracking goes by several names in literature and research on literacy, depending on what country the author is from and whether the focus is on primary grades, high school, or college. In this book, we define *tracking* as following a written text with eyes and often, a finger, while listening to the text read aloud. This technique has also been called *audio-assisted reading*, *immersive reading*, *reading while listening* (*RWL*), and *audio support*. In all cases, the student reads along silently while listening to the audio.

When first learning to track, following the text with a finger is especially helpful for students with dyslexia. Tracking can be done individually or in a group. The crucial element of tracking is that the reader is looking at the words as they hear them. At first, they trace under the words with their finger on the page, which helps with focus. As they become more practiced, they can visually follow the words on the page without using their finger.

Of all the tools in this book, Vicki feels that tracking has been the most crucial asset in her classroom. Easily confused with an elementary school technique of having students track with their finger under the words as they (often stressfully) read the text out loud, this tool puts the focus on relaxing and listening to the text while students track with their finger and train their eyes to follow the text.

The frustration of listening to a struggling, embarrassed student read out loud is gone for the whole class. Everyone can enjoy the text while the teacher can monitor who is actually keeping up when someone doesn't turn their page with the group. There is little embarrassment for students who fall behind as they are gently cued to catch up when everyone around them turns the page.

As outlined in the "Sample Tracking Lesson Plan" reproducible at the end of this chapter (page 93), Vicki taught this tool using repetition over short periods of time. She finds that teaching tracking with the finger and then giving students the freedom to track with their eyes after practicing with the finger helped them focus and comprehend the material better. Students were alert. No one fell asleep, as can happen when just the audio is played.

Tracking follows beautifully after teaching text-to-speech (chapter 1, page 23). Students already have access to numerous text-to-speech options they can use while tracking. In this chapter, we introduce programs such as Voice Dream Reader, Helperbird for Firefox, Microsoft's Immersive Reader, and the Immersive Reader Chrome extension, all of which have features specifically designed to support tracking for readers with dyslexia.

We find the Voice Dream Reader app especially useful. It was developed based on research that studied how successful readers with dyslexia use tracking (Warren, 2016). Voice Dream Reader supports many popular and growing multimedia file formats (DAISY, EPUB, PDF, MP3, HTML, and multiple Microsoft formats). Essentially, most text sources will work with it.

We find Voice Dream Reader helpful because it has the following features that are particularly useful for students with dyslexia.

- **Synchronized text-to-speech:** As each word is spoken out loud, that word is highlighted, helping the user match the visual word with its aural counterpart.

- **OpenDyslexic font:** According to OpenDyslexic (n.d.), this open-sourced font was "created to increase readability for readers with dyslexia" with the input of users who are dyslexic. Letters in the OpenDyslexic font are more heavily weighted at the bottom, which prevents the letters from "flying away" on the page as much.

- **Color options:** People with dyslexia have subtly different color preferences, so Voice Dream Reader lets each user choose from a massive palette of colors for text and background. This can reduce dyslexic disorientation.

- **Focused reading mode:** This reduces the size of the text area to prevent the eyes from wandering off the text. The text scrolls automatically so the spoken word is always in the middle of the screen.

- **Adjustable spacing between lines:** Adding white space between lines helps prevent the words appearing to overlap each other.

- **Adjustable margins:** When columns of print are less than about four inches across, readers with dyslexia have less trouble staying on the correct line.

- **Adjustable reading speed:** This allows readers to slowly increase the speed at which they track (Warren, 2016).

Students who find tracking helpful may want to invest in Voice Dream Reader or a similar app.

You certainly don't have time to teach students with dyslexia to read while also teaching mathematics, history, biology, or even literature. But, by teaching them how to track, you can give them a tool that helps them get the education they need and will align well with any reading intervention support a student might receive outside your class.

Tracking enables students who can't read yet to participate fully, access the content material, and avoid embarrassment, all while improving their reading skills. Let's take a look at the research on tracking. If you're looking for classroom ideas rather than research, feel free to skip the research section and dive straight into the subsequent section, Classroom Applications of Tracking (page 81).

How Tracking Helps Students With Dyslexia

An overview of the research on tracking reveals that outcomes for students who use it vary. Some research seems to show that tracking does not improve comprehension or retention of information (Clinton-Lisell, 2023; Zakiyuddin, Mustofa, & Yunus, 2022). Other studies point to dramatic improvements in comprehension for readers with dyslexia (Cubillas & Cangke, 2023; Elamadurthi et al., 2023; Knoop-van Campen, 2022; Wood et al., 2018).

The reason why there is such disparity in the research lies in how tracking is used. In her doctoral dissertation on tracking for dyslexia, Carolien A. N. Knoop-van Campen (2022) notes the following:

> As both decoding and working memory capacity impact cognitive load, learning in a multimedia environment could be particularly challenging for students with dyslexia. However, since audio-support [tracking] lowers the necessity to decode every single word and increases reading speed, audio could also lessen the cognitive load. In other words, audio-support could both hinder as well as aid learners with dyslexia. (p. 16)

In other words, adding audio to an already overstimulating visual component, such as a video or an ebook with pictures and other visuals, can have a negative impact, as the reader may cognitively try to do too much at once. However, when students use tracking to read plain text, they can concentrate more easily, keeping their eyes on the words being said. This allows for vocabulary and sight word recognition to increase over time as students hear and see words together in context.

Some studies (Clinton-Lisell, 2023; Zakiyuddin et al., 2022) tested student comprehension by presenting short informative paragraphs, often accompanied by visuals. Students were asked to read the passage either with or without audio voice-over. Since the students with audio had to keep up with the reader, they had no time to peruse the visuals or think about the material. These studies conclude that tracking did not improve comprehension for high school students, though it did for elementary students with dyslexia whose readings were less complex.

Other studies (Cubillas & Cangke, 2023; Elamadurthi et al., 2023; Knoop-van Campen, 2022; Wood et al., 2018) allowed students to use tracking for longer texts, such as chapters of novels or textbooks, that high school students might read. These studies focused on reading plain text rather than a text with accompanying visuals. If there were visuals, students could pause the narration to study them. These studies conclude that tracking raises the comprehension level of students with dyslexia to that of their peers without dyslexia.

Put simply, when readers with dyslexia practice tracking, their reading speed and comprehension increase and their reading vocabulary expands. As this occurs, some readers decide to bypass tracking in favor of going it on their own. Some take a highly creative approach by adjusting the voice speed to their new reading speed.

One example of this creative approach to reading comes from Matthew Schneps, an astrophysicist who is also a respected scientist in dyslexia research. Schneps started and directed the Laboratory for Visual Learning, a joint program of Harvard University and University of Massachusetts Boston for many years before it closed. Schneps realized that tracking is relatively slow, though not as slow as sounding out words, so he used technology to speed it up. An interview with Schneps by *Different Brains* (Reitman, 2016) explores his research.

Winston Chen, creator of the Voice Dream Reader app, writes about Schneps's use of tracking to keep up with the research papers in his field:

> [He] sets his text-to-speech rate to 650 words per minute. . . . To put that in perspective, on average people read visually at 200 words per minute and talk at 150 words per minute. . . . [Usually] only blind users of Voice Dream Reader can comprehend speech at 650 words per minute. . . . People with dyslexia have difficulty moving their attention forward as they read, and by using the word highlight to force their attention forward . . . reading speed improves. Second, people with dyslexia often get stuck on a word while trying to sound it out. But if the text-to-speech supplies the pronunciation for you, you can just move on rather than getting stuck. (Voice Dream, 2014)

Research into tracking generally doesn't include such highly efficient audio readers as Schneps in their experiments, since the research is usually done with high school students. However, researchers do recognize the spoken-word speed barrier. Carolien Knoop-van Campen points out that audio support (tracking) is no longer beneficial for efficient learning when reading becomes faster than speaking. However, for many high school students with dyslexia, that tipping point is still a long way off (Knoop-van Campen, 2022).

Knoop-van Campen (2022) concludes a rigorous meta-study of tracking in the high school classroom with this recommendation for publishers, students, and teachers:

> First, publishers and creators of educational materials should be motivated to include the possibility of audio-support [tracking] in their materials for children, as it decreases their study time. Second, learners who use audio-support should receive explanation and instruction about the possible impact audio-support can have on their learning process and outcomes. This way, they can learn how to use audio-support effectively. Finally, teachers can play an important role in supporting their students with regard to actively using the available audio-support. It is therefore recommended to incorporate the possibilities and drawbacks of audio-support in teacher education. (Knoop-van Campen, 2022, pp. 161–162)

To summarize the research on tracking: it is clear that this tool offers tremendous benefits to some students, especially those with dyslexia. It allows them to learn the informational content of their classes while simultaneously providing a means to improve their reading skills without outside help or embarrassment. The research is also clear that expecting students to track while also attending to graphs, pictures, or videos is counterproductive. Tracking must be done purposefully and in a focused manner, not just added on to an already overloaded brain.

Classroom Applications of Tracking

Students who don't read well by third grade miss a great deal of information that their peers pick up by reading (Redford, n.d.). Redford (n.d.) notes the following:

> Reading is harder and slower for dyslexic students. Consequently, they typically read less. If they are to keep up with their peers academically, then it is imperative to find additional ways to expose them to as many words and ideas as possible.

Reading builds on itself—the more a person reads, the better reader they become. Reading introduces literary vocabulary that nonreaders never encounter, which puts nonreaders at a huge disadvantage by high school. Students want to learn, and when they can't, they quickly approach the quitting point.

Tracking removes that roadblock and allows students with dyslexia to confidently participate in classroom discussions. Even more importantly, tracking has its greatest effect beyond the classroom as students adapt it to their own needs. The experience of a student named Richard illustrates how tracking is a tool that students can take outside the classroom to self-educate.

Richard is a cowboy. He grew up on a ranch in Colorado, and at the time Yvonna met him, he held a state title for roping and was working as a ranch hand. He also has dyslexia. At age sixteen, he couldn't read at all, and he was frustrated. His parents spent thousands of dollars on reading therapy, but it didn't move him forward as a reader.

Yvonna showed Richard how to use his iPad to hear and see text at the same time. He started tracking every night. His reading ability soared. After one year of daily tracking practice, he enrolled in GED classes. A few months later, he passed two of his GED tests. After more study, he passed the other tests and graduated.

Yvonna suggested that Richard start with easy books and work his way up to more difficult ones, but he ignored this advice. The first ebook he checked out of the library was *The Complete Works of Shakespeare* with audio option. He was hungry to know what other people read and talked about. It worked well to use headphones with his iPad in the bunkhouse at night. It didn't bother the other cowboys, and they thought he was listening to music, so he didn't have to explain anything. Returning from a ranch job in Wyoming, Richard told Yvonna, "That Shakespeare dude wrote some hilarious stuff."

Not every student will respond so dramatically to tracking, but the tool is versatile enough for any student to use as a life skill. Using the ideas in this chapter, you can offer this lifelong learning tool to every student in your classes.

Tracking not only allows students with dyslexia to keep up with the class readings but also actually sets students on a path that teaches them to read. Seeing and hearing the words simultaneously allows words and phrases to link in the brains of students with dyslexia, and in a way that uses their pattern-finding strength.

To offer this life-changing tech tool to your students, there's no need to rewrite your entire curriculum. Simply use the guidance in the following sections to add tracking as an option and show students how to access it.

Emphasize the Difference Between Tracking and Listening

When introducing students to tracking, it's vital to ensure they understand it's much more effective than just listening to an audiobook. While we love audiobooks and encourage students to enjoy them, listening doesn't address the reading issue. Visually tracking along the text while listening dramatically improves reading ability over time for most students, regardless of reading level (Reading Rockets, n.d.a).

Every student benefits from using tracking. Top students headed for Ivy League schools need to improve their vocabulary. Nonreaders need to read job applications. We hesitate to even mention testing, but increased vocabulary levels raise test scores in every subject area (Whitten, Labby, & Sullivan, 2016).

Redford (n.d.) suggests another benefit of tracking for students with dyslexia:

> Dyslexics often encounter a gap between their reading level and their intellectual level. This can turn them off of reading altogether. They don't want to read "baby books." Some handle this by faking engagement with thick sophisticated titles while others decide that they don't like to read at all and avoid it completely. Both can be disastrous responses.

Tracking is a way to expand vocabulary and is more fun and effective than worksheets. Let students know that everyone benefits regardless of how well they read or whether they read at all. Make it clear that listening to a book or watching a video is an excellent way to learn, no less worthy than traditional reading. Express the hope that your students will feel free to read, listen, or watch as they choose—these are equally valid ways of gaining knowledge. Emphasize that the best way to use these resources is to listen and look at the words simultaneously whenever possible. Acknowledge the central place that video and audio occupy in the future of learning.

Embed Tracking in Your Curriculum

Don't even think about overhauling your whole curriculum all at once. Take your time, using ideas from this chapter to make small changes as they suit you and your students' needs. Here are some ideas for incremental but powerful changes that empower your students with dyslexia.

- **Add paper copies to audiobooks:** If students are listening to an audiobook, put a copy of the paper book into their hands and show them how to follow along with the audio.

- **Turn on media subtitles or captions:** Students don't have to consciously read subtitles on videos, films, or other visual media. Seeing the words along with the spoken language will have a surprisingly strong effect as the subconscious mind starts pairing the spoken language with the written language. This is especially true for people with dyslexia. It's also helpful for English learners or students with hearing loss. Remind students to turn on subtitles at home when they watch movies. Numerous students with dyslexia have reported teaching themselves to read by playing video games that show the dialogue while the characters speak, which is another form of tracking (Université de Genève, 2022).

- **Take a quick poll:** Explain that tracking means seeing and hearing the words at the same time. Then, ask your students if any of them have ever done this. Let students share their experiences.

- **Predict possible problems:** Brainstorm with the class about possible difficulties that could arise while getting information via video or audio instead of traditional reading assignments. Pitfalls such as incorrect information, unreliable sources, ads that distract or are inappropriate, and not knowing where to look will probably come up naturally, but you can prompt as needed.

- **Focus the search:** Let your students find audio and video that can supplement or replace your reading assignments. Give the class specific keywords and phrases to look and listen for and let them do the searching. You've just covered essential vocabulary without sounding pedantic and sent them on a quest.

When the class meets next, discuss how closely the video and audio resources the students found meet the learning goals you targeted. Thank the students for their work. Do not grade them unless it's an A for everyone. Learning is its own reward. Grades can, unfortunately, remove the motivation to find information and replace it with the motivation to get a grade.

Build a Curriculum-Aligned Digital and Physical Multimedia Library

Every time you teach a unit, you'll probably add resources that support tracking. Soon, it will be quick to put together lesson plans. Over time, you'll be able to build up digital and physical resources that you can easily access to support your students. Organize these resources in your computer and in your classroom in a way that makes sense to you so you don't waste time looking for them.

For digital resources, tag every file with keywords such as *tracking*, *vocabulary*, or *cell structure*. This helps build searchable resource folders for each class, lesson, or unit. In your physical classroom space, build a library of paper books that pair up with the audiobooks you use. Students are much more likely to dive into tracking if both the paper book and the audiobook are readily available.

Of course, you won't have all of this organized and on hand immediately. Transitioning to a tracking-friendly classroom takes time, so do it in small steps, with students helping to locate the best materials. Some of these audio and video resources will be useful in more than one class or unit, so make copies as needed. That way, you aren't searching for a missing video. You'll have everything in one basket. This will also make it easy to leave a plan for a substitute teacher.

Most high school classes end up being perfectly paced—for one subset of students. For the rest, it's either too slow or too fast. Videos and audiobooks let students replay, repeat, or speed through. Good readers can still get the material from a book or article. Now, the focus is on the learning objectives instead of how many pages you assign. Meanwhile, you've just met some important IEP goals without adding to your workload.

Seek Buy-In From Others in the School

Your students will benefit from having tracking resources in every class. The more teachers in your building who offer this, the better for the students. Of course, you won't get very far by trying to force or manipulate change, but it's well established that teacher collaboration is among the most powerful drivers of improved student learning outcomes (DuFour, DuFour, Eaker, Many, Mattos, & Muhammad, 2024). Just mentioning what you're doing and what's worked well goes a long, long way with your colleagues.

Also, the school librarian may be your best ally. Let the librarian know what you are doing and why and ask about resources that would facilitate your transition to trackable audio and video lessons. Brainstorming with a librarian can pay huge dividends.

Start a Tracking Tradition

Perhaps once a week, set aside time for the class to listen to an audiobook together while tracking along in a paper book or printout. It's a lovely downtime for you and a bonding experience for the students. If you enjoy reading aloud, you can of course do the audio yourself. If possible, let students move around and get comfortable so they can thoroughly enjoy the reading.

If you teach language arts, you can choose a teen-friendly novel to spark discussion. If you are a history teacher, it's a great way to introduce important change makers of the past. For science classes, a biography of a scientist, such as Albert Einstein, who many believe had dyslexia, can bring the subject to life.

Tracking sessions need to be relaxed and fun. That means you don't need to grade for participation or try to analyze who is keeping their eyes on the paper. If most students are tracking well enough to stay on the right page, all is well. They'll all get better at it with practice. The beauty of this approach is that everyone is participating in the activity together. It's far more effective than singling out the poor readers and telling them to do it by themselves.

This is also a chance to model tracking. Students who get lost can watch you turn the page, so they can find their place. For a long reading, stop every two or three pages and let everyone know what page the reader is on, so they can find it if they need to.

Make Your Own Videos

When and if you want to, you can take tracking to the next level and make your own videos with subtitles. That sounds difficult. However, it's probably easier than you think. Ask a student volunteer to use their phone to film you explaining a key concept in the upcoming lesson. Have the student send you the video. Post it to your class website if you have one. Or post it to YouTube if you have a channel.

Someone in your class probably knows how to make and share videos, and this is their chance to shine. Maybe that student will even set up a YouTube channel for you. Another student may know how to edit the subtitles that YouTube generates automatically but not perfectly. Yvonna learned this skill from her high school–age granddaughter. Keep your videos concise. Don't worry about perfection. It won't be perfect, and that's OK. Your students are exposed to endless professionally produced videos. What will get their attention is a video you made yourself, just for them. As you get better at this, you can replace videos as you choose.

Because it's you on the video, the students still feel connected even when you aren't personally talking to them. There's no need to get fancier, but if you find you enjoy the video world, you can step up your game to make interactive videos. Visit Edpuzzle (https://edpuzzle.com) to see what's possible.

The beauty of making your own videos with subtitles is that students who don't read can watch these videos as many times as they need to start filling in those holes that come with avoiding text. An added benefit is that those videos are now part of your resources for future classes. You can use them over and over. These videos can save you a huge amount of time.

This doesn't mean you send your students off into videoland and hope they survive. Instead, it means you don't have to repeat yourself endlessly. Now, you'll have more time and energy to answer questions. You have time to discuss what they are learning and guide them toward mature use of learning resources. In short, you'll have time to connect with students as human beings in a supportive role.

Record Your Textbook

When selecting a textbook for your program, check with the publishing company to see if they have audio versions available. If your state or district is in the process of choosing curriculum materials, contact them and request that they also look for materials that include audio support.

If you use a paper textbook and have time, you can make audio recordings of each chapter and make these available to all students. Here again, a student can help you with this if you don't have the time or tech skills needed. A student may even volunteer to record the textbook themselves. Audio textbooks are also available from Learning Ally (https://learningally.org), which offers excellent options for schools and districts.

It's possible that drama or speech students would be glad to produce some of the audio or video resources you need. The instructors in these classes may be happy to have real-world assignments to give their students, as it adds motivation and meaning to their work.

Although it takes time up front, your voice, or that of a classmate, on the recording provides a connection for students. The voice paired with the text or the subtitles forges a connection between spoken and written vocabulary and is far more interesting than listening to a stranger. As teachers know, the relationship between reader and listener is what drives the learning. It's not about how professional your recording sounds.

Save Teacher Time Too

It's our expectation from experience that using the various audio supports discussed in this chapter will result in saving you time rather than adding to your load. By building a personal library of audio recordings and subtitled videos, keyed to your particular classes, you can quickly guide students to resources they need to master concepts in your class. You can easily put together a lesson or review of anything you've taught before. You can also quickly put together appropriate resources for your substitute when needed.

How to Address Pushback From Naysayers

Hopefully, you will have no need to defend your classroom choices to anyone—but if you do, here are a few common concerns you may hear from other educators or student caregivers.

"It's hard to get audio textbooks and I don't have time to record."

You're right. It can be a real pain to get audio textbooks. If you don't want to make a recording, that's OK. It's not necessary as part of providing video and audio resources for students. You can easily stay connected in other ways such as group discussions of YouTube videos with subtitles you watch together as a class.

What about asking for student volunteers to record chapters of the textbook? This involves students who are good readers and takes the burden of recording off your shoulders. You and your students get all the benefits with very little of your time spent.

"Listening to books will make students lazy and they'll never learn to read."

The research shows exactly the opposite. Using audiobooks along with text actually raises reading level, vocabulary, and reading motivation for poor readers. Students who are offered the option of audio support tend to read more, not less (Gorelik, 2017). It's a win for everyone.

Great teachers meet the students where they are, not where they think they should be. And it's certain that required readings alone will not teach students to read. So, it makes sense to pave the way to maximum learning for all students.

"It takes longer to listen to a book than to read it."

This is true of fast readers. However, readers with dyslexia often read very slowly, if at all—much more slowly than they speak because they are sounding out words (Shaywitz, 2020). The average English speaker talks at about 150 words per minute (Baruch College, n.d.). According to Weitzman (2022a), a standard audiobook is typically narrated at a pace of about 150 to 160 words per minute. So, tracking with an audiobook actually saves time for most dyslexic high school students. After students learn to track, they often speed up the audio, saving even more time. Fast readers may opt to read the book without the audio, and that's fine. Students will tend to use the tools that work best for them.

"There's no way I can tell if the students are really tracking."

Very true. You can have students move their fingers along the lines or down the middle or side of the page as they follow the reader. This will help you pick up on any students having difficulty. If you are practicing the tool in the classroom with a group of students, you will notice whether someone is not turning the page with the rest of the class. This also gives the individual student a chance to discreetly and safely get caught up if they have lost their place by noticing when the class turns the page.

Once students get good at tracking, the finger may just get in the way. This is a time to celebrate when a student doesn't feel the need to use their finger and is able to track easily using just their eyes.

The goal of tracking is to make it a tool students use on their own whenever it helps them to fully comprehend a text, so overcontrolling is counterproductive. You want to hand them the tool, be sure they know how to use it, then get out of their way and let them decide when and how they use it.

Summary

In this summary section, we offer a quick list of the main points covered in this chapter, followed by questions for reflection. We also include a sample lesson plan for introducing tracking into your classroom (page 93).

It's designed to make it easy to link tracking instruction time to existing standards and IEP and 504 goals.

- Tracking means reading along silently while listening to the text being read aloud.

- Tracking allows students with dyslexia to comprehend text at the same level as their nondyslexic peers.

- Contrary to a persistent educational myth, tracking increases rather than decreases the amount of reading students do, thus increasing their vocabulary and background knowledge.

- Tracking saves time for teachers because audio resources reduce prep time and provide easy options for substitute teachers or yourself.

Reflection

Use the following questions to further consider this chapter's new tool and how you can use it to help struggling readers.

1. How might you introduce tracking in your classroom? What do you think the student response will be?

2. What might tracking help you learn about your students?

3. Have you used any sort of audio supports in your classroom before? How did it go?

4. How might tracking benefit the struggling readers in your classroom? How might it benefit the stronger readers?

5. What would you tell another teacher about using tracking to support learners with dyslexia?

Reproducible Forms With Suggested Standards and IEP and 504 Goals

When you use tracking in your classroom, you meet multiple state standards, IEP goals, 504 accommodations, and various inclusion requirements. The reproducible "Sample Tracking Lesson Plan" is intended for the entire class, as this tool can be beneficial to any student. It's a great way to get every student reading more and trying new tools.

Sample Tracking Lesson Plan

Unit or Topic: Tracking

Days: Five (ten minutes per day for five days)

Content Standards	
List the standards applicable to this unit or topic: CCSS.ELA-Literacy.CCRA.R.2—Determine central ideas or themes of a text and analyze their development; summarize the key supporting details and ideas.	
Content Objectives: What are students learning? Students are learning how to track text on a page while reading text listening to a recording of a text.	**Language Objectives:** How will students learn it? For five or ten minutes a day over a five-day period, students will listen to a piece of text read aloud while they track the words on the written page using their finger. They will determine and summarize the text's central idea or theme.
Essential Questions: How does tracking work while using audio-assisted reading?	**Bloom's Taxonomy:** Check those that apply. The essential question is . . . ✓ Low (Knowledge and Comprehension) ✓ Middle (Application and Analysis) ✓ High (Synthesis and Evaluation) ✓ Psychomotor (Physical Speed and Accuracy)
Building Background	
Prior Knowledge: What do students need to know before the lesson? No prior knowledge is needed.	
Key Vocabulary: audio-assisted reading, tracking	

Lesson Delivery

Instructional Time: Approximately ten minutes (Depending on the class length, decide whether a five- or ten-minute lesson is best suited for the class. This lesson plan is based on ten minutes.)

Lesson Sequence:

Day 1

1. Explain to students what tracking is, and that research has shown that it can improve their reading. Also explain the following.
    a. It may feel awkward at first, like learning a new dance, so it is important that students not judge the technique until they give it some time and practice.
    b. They are only going to practice for ten minutes each day over a five-day period because repetition will make it more comfortable.
    c. At the end of the five days, students can choose whether they want to continue tracking on their own. Tell them you just need their cooperation for five days to give it a chance.
    d. Point out that it may not be that easy to follow along and, if they get lost, they don't have to say anything. They should just listen to the reading but notice when everyone turns a page. That will be their cue to turn their page and catch up and start tracking again.
2. Demonstrate the technique. Show students how they can follow the text with their finger in different ways.
    a. Word by word: Follow each word across the sentence in a straight line.
    b. *S* movement: Follow the text by smoothly moving the finger down the page in multiple *S* movements.
3. Practice the technique. Set the timer for ten minutes and start audio of the text. Walk around the room to watch students move their fingers down the page so they know that you are paying close attention to them. If possible, carry the text with you and model the movements with your own finger.
4. Notice if someone is not turning the page when everyone else turns a page. They are either not motivated or getting lost. Either way, don't single them out unless they ask for help. Just stay positive and compliment the group for doing a good job following along. Remind them that their brain is trying something new and it will get easier. (Don't be surprised if the nonmotivated students sound disgruntled and lack movement. They are watching and taking note. Surprisingly, they may practice this on their own.)
5. Have students write down a sentence or two telling what the reading was about.
6. Have students write down their thoughts and feelings about using this technique today. Have them save this writing for a later discussion.

Never Too Late © 2025 Solution Tree Press • SolutionTree.com
Visit **go.SolutionTree.com/literacy** to download this free reproducible.

Days 2–5

1. Practice the technique. Set the timer for ten minutes and start audio of the text. Watch students move their fingers down the page to follow.
2. Praise, praise, praise. Remind students that performing the movements with the text is all that is expected of them.
3. Have students write down a sentence or two telling what the reading was about.
4. Have students write down their thoughts and feelings about using this technique today.
5. Be open to discussing how tracking is working for them, but resist getting into long discussions. In fact, handling it with a "this is just what we do" attitude and quickly moving into the day's lesson can take out the mystery and make it more comfortable for everyone. Tell them that day 5 can include a longer discussion.

Once you feel students have consistently used the word-by-word or *S* movements, introduce the margin movement: Trackers move their finger down the margin of the page instead of following word for word or in an *S* movement. (Don't introduce this option on day 1. Students will default to this option without trying the other options, as it feels easier to them. Meanwhile, they won't experience the other options that actually help them "see" the words as they are spoken.)

Closure:

Day 5

1. After practicing, congratulate the class for doing a good job.
2. Remind students that it is now optional to use.
3. Have students silently write down their thoughts on learning this tool and compare it to what they wrote on day 1. Do this before having a class discussion.
4. Discuss the students' reactions, comments, and questions as a whole class.
5. Consider sharing the research findings (presented in chapter 3, page 73) supporting why this tool can help improve their reading.
6. Discuss where they can find audio recordings for the class texts (if available).
7. Brainstorm where and how they can get recordings for other readings they do in their life.
8. Discuss how using the text-to-speech apps may enable them to get the audio version of almost anything they want to read.

Don't be surprised if students indicate they want to continue the ten-minute sessions.

Materials and Supplies:
- For students, a notebook, sheet of paper, or other way to write down or record responses as notes that they will use each day
- A short piece of text to read aloud each day; this might be a section of the required reading for each day's class
- A timer, such as a stopwatch or the timer on a cell phone—anything that would have an audible sound at the end of the ten minutes

Also consider:
- If possible, select text that does not have visually distracting ads or graphics.
- Read something from current news that is or is not related to the class content.
- Use an additional resource for the curriculum. For example, in a science class, each day could be a different current-event discovery in the science world.
- Choose selections from the text that you might include on an upcoming test.
- **Note:** Depending on the material you choose for this activity, your class could meet more of the instructional strategies listed later than what is already indicated on this lesson plan.

WICOR (Writing, Inquiry, Collaboration, Organization, and Reading) Strategies

Depending on the school district, the following instructional strategy responses may be required for a lesson plan. This section includes definitions and sample activities that a district may not provide but could be useful.

Check all that apply and then underline the activity in that category.

- ✓ **Writing** (prewrite, draft, respond, revise, edit, final draft, <u>class and textbook notes</u>, learning logs)
- ✓ **Inquiry** (Costa's levels of questions, <u>skilled questioning</u>, Socratic seminars, <u>quick writes and discussion</u>, <u>critical thinking activities</u>, writing questions, <u>open-mindedness activities</u>)
- __ **Collaboration** (group projects, study groups, jigsaw activities, response-edit-revision activities, collaborative activities)
- __ **Organization** (tools such as binders, calendars, planners, agendas, graphic organizers, and methods such as focused note-taking system, tutorials, study groups, project planning)
- ✓ **Reading** (SQ3R method [survey, <u>question</u>, <u>read</u>, recite, <u>review</u>], KWL charts [what I know, what I want to learn, what I learned], reciprocal teaching, think-alouds, <u>reader response</u>, graphic organizers, vocabulary building)

Strategies

Check any or all that apply.

Scaffolding:	Describe here if needed:	Concept Development:
✔ Modeling ✔ Guided Practice — Independent Practice		— Similarities and Differences — Summarizing and Note-Taking ✔ Reinforcing Effort and Providing Recognition — Nonlinguistic Representation — Generating and Testing Hypotheses
Practice and Application: ✔ Listening ✔ Reading — Worksheet — Writing — Discussion ✔ Hands-On or Manipulatives		
Interaction: ✔ Whole Class — Small Group — Partners — Independent	**5E Lesson Planning:** ✔ Engage (capture interest) ✔ Explore (experiment, simulate, or collaborate) — Explain (discuss and define concepts) — Elaborate (apply new knowledge) ✔ Evaluate (assess to gauge comprehension)	**Engaging Qualities:** — Personal Response ✔ Clear and Modeled Expectations — Emotional and Intellectual Safety ✔ Learning With Others — Sense of Audience — Choice ✔ Novelty and Variety — Authenticity

Special Education Requirements

Accommodations—How to Instruct
(to make education more accessible for students with disabilities)

Examples: Timing and scheduling for classwork and tests; reduced-distraction setting; special equipment; presentation in large print; recorded or human-read books; responses using a scribe, graphic organizer, calculator, or speech-to-text equipment

Modifications—What to Instruct
(only for students with an IEP)

Examples: Use fewer concepts, ask different test questions, reduce number of problems, revise assignments, give hints or clues, modify tests, grade on effort, use alternative text and assignments, modify questions, shorten assignments, give open-book tests

Consider each of the following instructional areas. Where appropriate, describe the activity and check whether it was an accommodation or modification.

Instructional Area	Activity	Accommodation	Modification
Content	Students will have fewer visual distractions.	✓	
Materials	Students will be given printed text paired with text audio.	✓	
Delivery	Teacher will read aloud while teaching students how to track.	✓	
Activity	Students will track using printed text.	✓	

Review and Assessment

Consider the following questions before choosing the assessment:
- How will students receive feedback?
- How do students know what is expected of them?

Check all that apply and provide a brief description.

✓ Formative assessment (*for* learning; informal)

Examples: Identifying where students are and what their needs are, applying questioning strategies, using exit tickets, checking in with students

Identify where the students are by asking the following questions: What problems did they have learning or practicing the technique? Was their experience of using the technique on day 1 different from day 5? Was it the same? Why?

___ Summative assessment (*of* learning; formal)

Examples: Grading, tests, quizzes, performance tasks, rubrics

Reflection

What do you need to change to facilitate improvement?

What will you do differently if students have not demonstrated mastery of the objective?

What would you add?

Specific things to consider on this tracking lesson:

Check the teacher's attitude: Is the teacher's attitude one of enthusiasm and support when presenting the tool? This is a powerful tool that can change the life of a student with dyslexia and should be seen that way.

Reflect on time provided:
Did students have enough time to practice using the tool? Why or why not?

Source: AVID. (n.d.). WICOR (writing, inquiry, collaboration, organization, and reading). *Accessed at https://avidopenaccess.org/wp-content/uploads/2021/08/AVID-WICOR-flyer-080521_proofed.pdf on July 24, 2024; Echevarría, J., Vogt, M., Short, D. J., & Toppel, K. (2024).* Making content comprehensible for multilingual learners: The SIOP model (6th ed.). *Pearson; Gerges, E. (2022, March 4).* How to use the 5E model in your science classroom. *Edutopia. Accessed at www.edutopia.org/article/how-use-5e-model-your-science-classroom on April 9, 2024; Idaho Special Education Support & Technical Assistance (SESTA). (2022).* Idaho IEP guidance handbook: High-quality practices. *Accessed at https://idahotc.com /Portals/0/Resources/1007/The-Idaho-IEP -Guidance-Handbook.pdf on April 9, 2024; National Governors Association Center for Best Practices & Council of Chief State School Officers. (2010).* Common Core State Standards for English language arts and literacy in history/social studies, science, and technical subjects. *Authors. Accessed at https://corestandards.org/wp-content /uploads/2023/09/ELA_Standards1.pdf on January 5, 2025.*

CHAPTER 4

Using Headphones as an Educational Support

> One of my students performed a radical, poetic intervention into that field of isolation. He was listening to music with headphones, sitting next to a woman also wearing headphones, who was moving a little to her music. He took off his headphones and held them out to her. She looked puzzled for a moment, then took hers off and traded with him. They listened to each other's music for a few minutes and then traded back. Not a word passed between them.
> —KIO STARK

At sixteen, Alex strides through life taking charge. She's tall, friendly, and smart. What could possibly get in her way?

Noise.

High school was turning into a nightmare for Alex. She was missing around ten days a month due to migraines, which sent her to bed for a day or two at a time. Her parents took her to multiple doctors and she tried increasingly strong medications, some not recommended for teenagers. The migraines always started at school, never at home. She was desperate for an answer.

Thanks to parents who relentlessly worked on the problem and a school nurse who cared, everything changed for Alex in her sophomore year. She learned that she is highly sensitive to noise and light. She sees the flicker in fluorescent lighting and hears noise at much higher frequencies than most people. The school environment produced sensory overload that brought on migraines. Her high school thankfully replaced the lighting with LED as part of an energy-saving program. Her parents purchased high-quality noise-canceling headphones for her. The nurse convinced the administration and teachers that the headphones were a medical necessity for Alex.

Alex would soon happily use her headphones in the hallway, at lunch, and any time she didn't need to be listening to the teacher in class. Migraine frequency diminished, and she quickly went off all the troublesome medications. Sometimes, the answer to a problem is so simple it's easy to miss.

In this chapter, we consider the use of headphones as a valuable educational tool. We will discuss different types of headphones, hearing protection, background noise, signal-to-noise ratio, focus and attention, and music for study.

What Headphones Do

Headphones don't need much description, though there are different forms of headphone technology. Teachers don't need to be headphone experts, but it helps to know that not all headphones are alike and what specific features might do in an educational context, especially if you are on the committee that's deciding what to purchase for your school. The following list (House of Marley, 2023) provides an overview of some types of headphones or features, more than one of which may be present on a given set of headphones.

- **Over-ear headphones (circumaural):** These headphones feature large ear cups that enclose the ears fully.

- **On-ear headphones (supra-aural):** On-ear headphones, or supra-aural headphones, provide a middle ground between the over-ear and earbud style. They rest comfortably on the outer ear, providing a comfortable fit without fully enclosing the ear. This design offers a balanced, natural sound quality while maintaining a relatively compact size.

- **Earbuds:** Earbuds fit inside the outer ear. They are compact, lightweight, and easy to carry around.

- **In-ear monitors:** Often used by musicians and audio engineers, in-ear monitors (IEMs) are inserted directly into the ear canal. The tight seal they form effectively blocks out external noise.

- **Wireless (Bluetooth) headphones:** These headphones, which can be earbuds or fit on or over the ears, connect your devices without the constraints of cables and wires.

- **Noise-canceling headphones:** Headphones that have this feature have microphones that capture the surrounding sounds and then generate the opposite sound waves to cancel them out. This process is called active noise cancellation (ANC).

- **Bone conduction headphones:** This type of headphone rests "directly on the listener's cheekbones. Unlike traditional headphones and earbuds, the eardrum doesn't vibrate to pass the information along to the cochlea. Instead, the vibrations from the bone conduction bee-lines for the cochlea" (Katz, 2024). These innovative headphones deserve a mention for their intriguing functionality, particularly because they are specifically beneficial to individuals with hearing impairments or those who want to keep their ears open to external sounds.

- **Closed-back headphones:** Closed-back headphones feature sealed ear cups that prevent sound from escaping or entering the headphones. This design creates a more immersive and isolated listening experience.

- **Open-back headphones:** On the other end of the spectrum, open-back headphones have ear cups with perforations or grilles that allow sound to escape and external sound to enter. This design creates a more natural soundstage. Students wearing this type of headphone may truthfully tell you that they can hear you with their headphones on. Nevertheless, we think removing headphones when a teacher is speaking shows good manners and is good practice for the classroom.

- **Semi-open headphones:** Semi-open headphones strike a balance between the isolation of closed-back headphones and the openness of open-back headphones. They provide a more natural sound reproduction while still offering some degree of sound isolation. Semi-open headphones are worth considering if you desire a blend of immersive audio and ambient sound awareness

We all know what headphones are. However, awareness of these headphone features will help you answer the question, "Do headphones contribute to or detract from student success in high school classrooms, especially for students with dyslexia?" Let's dig into the research on headphone use in schools. If you're looking for classroom ideas rather than research, feel free to skip the research section and dive straight into the subsequent section, Classroom Applications of Headphones (page 114).

How Headphones Help Students With Dyslexia

Before we address how specific headphone features support learning for students with dyslexia, we need to step back and think about the noise levels of school environments as well as noise levels that are safe in headphones.

Educators, with good reason, often bring up the danger of headphones and hearing damage. This prompts us to ask, "How loud is too loud?" The Center for Hearing and Communication (n.d.) posts this warning: "To know if a sound is loud enough to cause damage to your ears, it is important to know both the level of intensity (measured in decibels, dBA) and the length of exposure to the sound." Soft dB (2019), a company that produces sound-masking technology, explains the impact of decibels on the human ear:

> A dBA is a weighted scale for judging loudness that corresponds to the hearing threshold of the human ear. Although dB is commonly used when referring to measuring sound, humans do not hear all frequencies equally. For this reason, sound levels in the low frequency end of the spectrum are reduced as the human ear is less sensitive at low audio frequencies than at high audio frequencies.

In general, the louder the sound, the less time required before hearing will be affected. Continued exposure to noise above 85 dBA will eventually harm your hearing. Examples of noise at 85 dBA include a food blender, a truck passing, or the inside of an airport. The Occupational Safety and Health Administration (n.d.) takes noise exposure seriously:

> Exposure to loud noise kills the nerve endings in our inner ear. More exposure will result in more dead nerve endings. The result is permanent hearing loss that cannot be corrected through surgery or with medicine. Noise-induced hearing loss limits your ability to hear high-frequency sounds and understand speech, which seriously impairs your ability to communicate. Hearing aids may help, but they do not restore your hearing to normal.

On the other hand, responsible headphone usage can protect hearing. Blogger Sienna Smith (2021) explains the following:

> It might sound counterproductive to use classroom headsets to protect children's hearing. . . . In contrast, consistently exposing a child to loud environments does have the potential to damage their hearing. [Headphones] can prevent a child from constantly being exposed to a noisy environment such as a classroom.

Since classroom noise varies and student tolerance of noise varies, we looked for research on average high school classroom noise levels. Lily M. Wang and Laura C. Brill (2021) present research into sound levels in K–12 classrooms in the United States. As you might expect, kindergarten through third-grade classrooms are generally louder when averaged over a full day than grades 4–12 classrooms. In their findings, grades 3 and 8 experienced the most sound spikes over 65 dBA. Wang and Brill (2021) explain how they gathered this information:

> Sound levels were processed to estimate occupied [classroom] signal-to-noise ratios (SNRs), using Gaussian mixture modeling and from daily equivalent and statistical levels.... The SNRs calculated as the daily difference between the average levels for the speech and non-speech [background noise] clusters are found to be lower than 15 dB in 27.3% of the classrooms.... Finally, classroom speech and non-speech levels were significantly correlated, with a 0.29 dBA increase in speech levels for every 1 dBA in non-speech levels. (p. 864)

That's a lot of technical information, so we're going to unpack the part that's important for teachers.

First, it's good news that overall sound levels in U.S. classrooms tended to be within the safe range below 85 dBA. This, however, doesn't tell the entire story. As we seek to make our classrooms more supportive of students with dyslexia, one of Wang and Brill's (2021) findings is especially important: the signal-to-noise ratio.

When the base level of noise (background noise) is high, the audio signal that carries pertinent information (the teacher's voice, for example) can be easily lost or misheard by listeners with dyslexia, as Tilde Van Hirtum, Pol Ghesquière, and Jan Wouters (2021) show in the *Journal of the Association for Research in Otolaryngology*. The challenge for a classroom teacher is to maintain a signal-to-noise ratio high enough for students with dyslexia to understand the teacher's voice or other audio material without exceeding safe total noise levels.

Van Hirtum and colleagues (2021) measured at what signal-to-noise ratio students with dyslexia lose the signal in the noise. They compare this to the point at which nondyslexic listeners can no longer distinguish signal from noise. Students with dyslexia lose the ability to distinguish the teacher's voice or presentation sooner than other students. This means that even when most of the class can hear and understand the teacher, students with dyslexia with normal hearing may hear the teacher speaking but are unable to distinguish the teacher's words from the background noise.

High school students with dyslexia are unlikely to understand why they are missing things and certainly won't self-advocate if everyone else seems to understand what's going on. Thankfully, high school classroom teachers don't need noise meters and other expensive equipment to assess background noise and signal-to-noise ratio. The Occupational Safety and Health Administration (n.d.) provides an easy way to estimate background noise level: "If you need to raise your voice to speak to someone three feet away, noise levels might be over 85 decibels."

Since we know from Wang and Brill (2021) that background noise in U.S. high schools tends to be around 65 dBA, we need not be concerned about background noise unless the situation is unusual, such as a school near an airport. What we must address is the signal-to-noise ratio, thus making sure our students with dyslexia can clearly hear what goes on in the classroom. That's where headphones may play a part.

Noise-canceling headphones reduce the background noise, allowing students to listen to the informative voice at a lower, safer level. Rather than measuring noise levels, the teacher provides access and permission to use headphones and observes which students and how many students make use of the tool.

If observation suggests that students may need a better signal-to-noise ratio, then teachers might consider moving more instruction to headphone-accessible media (audiobooks, teacher-recorded videos, and so on). The key for teachers is knowing that students with dyslexia may lose the signal before the rest of the class, so the teacher can be alert to possible needs for headphone accessibility.

We know that background noise above 85 dBA over time can cause hearing damage, and headphones can help with both background noise and signal-to-noise ratio, but headphones can also produce noise that's too loud to be safe. It's only reasonable to be sure students understand this danger. It doesn't take long to go over rules for responsible and safe headphone use, an example of which you'll find later in this chapter (page 118).

Headphone Usage Will Differ From Student to Student

As we dig deeper into the research surrounding headphone usage in classrooms, we find it important to consider this observation from researcher Pawel R. Kulawiak (2021) at the University of Potsdam's Department of Inclusive Education:

> The academic benefits of wearing noise-canceling headphones may depend on different noise conditions (sound level, environmental noise, irrelevant speech, etc.), individual differences among students (age, types and severity of special needs, abilities, etc.), and types of academic performance (recall, reading comprehension, task difficulty, form of learning, etc.). (p. 16)

In other words, never assume that what's beneficial for one student automatically meets the needs of another. Likewise, what a student needs for one task may differ from their needs for a different task.

Having your high school students practice responsible use of headphones will benefit them when they head for college. University students with dyslexia may find that headphones enhance their ability to focus on their studies. For example, the Yale Center for Dyslexia & Creativity (n.d.c) has a webpage called *Tips From Students*. While this is not research in the stringent sense, it is important information from students with dyslexia who are managing the study requirements at Yale University. Among other great tips, the students mention, "Work in a quiet place with few distractions. Ear plugs or noise-canceling headphones can help to block out noises that compete for your attention."

Headphones Allow Students With Dyslexia to Enjoy Reading for Pleasure

It's easy to overlook reading for pleasure in discussing dyslexia in the high school classroom. Students with dyslexia often avoid reading except when it's necessary to pass a class or succeed at a task. However, we know that students who read more gain background information, learn more vocabulary, and test better. These advantages don't need to be reserved for good readers, since tracking offers dyslexic learners the same benefits (chapter 3, page 73).

What does pleasure reading have to do with headphones? Everything. High school students will certainly not do independent tracking without headphones—it's rude to others and embarrassing to the reader. If the headphones are of good quality, the reading pleasure increases. Reading for pleasure is arguably more important than reading an assignment, because it enhances life beyond the school years.

Researchers Christy Whitten, Sandra Labby, and Sam L. Sullivan (2016) summarize the benefits of making pleasure reading accessible for students with dyslexia:

> Educators are frequently looking for new and innovative ways to improve student performance in the classroom. Substandard writing skills, poor reading comprehension skills, low-level vocabulary, and lackluster scores on standardized tests are legitimate concerns in many school districts. . . . [Our research] concluded that students who chose to read self-selected literature for pleasure performed better in English, mathematics, science, and history. (p. 58)

Our students with dyslexia often need headphones to read for pleasure.

Allowing students with dyslexia to listen to music on their headphones may increase their ability to focus, relax, and study. National University (n.d.) notes that "Music activates both the left and right brain at the same time, and the activation of both hemispheres can maximize learning and improve memory." The National University article goes on to mention that music can positively affect our mood, blood pressure, and heart rate. For students with dyslexia who find school a stressful environment, music breaks with headphones may be a key to a better school experience.

National University (n.d.), drawing on a 2007 research study by scholars at the Stanford School of Medicine (Stanford Medicine, 2007), suggests that students choose tunes that keep them awake but won't cause them to start shimmying and tapping to the beat. Rather than relying on the radio or a random mix on Pandora or Spotify, it can help to create a playlist of the best study music for concentration. Students can plan a set amount of uninterrupted music, which serves as a built-in timer for studying. When the music is up, you've earned a break.

A National University (n.d.) blog for student success provides the following list of great tips for using music to study:

> - Consider the tempo: Music with 60–70 beats per minute, like Beethoven's "Für Elise," appears to help students study longer and retain more information.
> - Sound control: The volume of your study music is key. Don't drown out your own thoughts. Remember, it's supposed to be in the background.
> - Avoid music with lyrics: Songs that tempt us to sing along or ponder the meaning of the lyrics tend to distract more than help.
> - Find commercial-free music: Avoid music with commercials and incessant DJ chatter, which are added distractions that pull your attention away from the task at hand.
> - Choose something you like: For the most benefits, listen to music you enjoy, and that makes you feel good. A recent study suggests memory is improved by the mood boost from listening, not the background music itself. (National University, n.d.)

Remember that not everyone studies better with music. Try it, and honestly assess whether it helps or hinders you. If it distracts, but you love music, use music as a reward for yourself after a study session.

To wrap up our review of research on headphone use, we revisit and summarize the work of Van Hirtum and colleagues (2021). These researchers show that students with dyslexia have low ability to hear clearly with background noise. When exposed to learning materials with headphones and enhanced envelope (EE) audio, students' ability to accurately understand spoken speech improved immediately. *Enhanced envelope* refers to enhancing the highs and lows of speech, emphasizing the intonation and verbal cues most of us take for granted but which listeners with dyslexia may miss (Van Hirtum et al., 2021).

Van Hirtum and colleagues (2021) conclude the following:

> Our results confirm the presence of poor speech perception in noise in school-aged children with dyslexia. Moreover, the presence of these deficits in both school-aged children and adults indicate that speech perception difficulties persist over time.... More importantly, our results demonstrated that emphasizing amplitude rise times in speech using EE instantaneously improved speech perception in children with dyslexia. The same benefit was also found in adults with dyslexia. (p. 465)

This means that headphones will benefit your students with dyslexia any time they need to listen carefully.

While high school teachers won't be using EE techniques with their students with dyslexia, they can offer the next best thing. They can give permission to use noise-canceling headphones, thus removing a large part of the cognitive load under which students with dyslexia struggle. This simple tool can make a tremendous positive difference for such students.

As headphone and earbud technology continues to evolve, remarkable tools arise. For example, on National Public Radio, Juliana Kim (2024) reviews Apple AirPods, which are marketed as combination earbuds and hearing aids. Our students with dyslexia probably don't need hearing aids, but users can program these Apple AirPods via an app on their phone to lower some noises and increase others. Students could use this to lower background noise and enhance the teacher's voice. This is amazing and exciting for students with dyslexia as well as those with hearing loss.

A review of Apple AirPods Pro 2 by Nicky Chong-White, Jorge Mejia, and Brent Edwards, (2023), researchers at the National Acoustic Laboratories in Sydney, Australia, describes how perfectly this new technology may meet the dyslexic need to dampen background noise in order to focus in class:

> It should be noted that for live conversations in noisy environments, other hearing features, like Headphone Accommodations, Ambient Noise Reduction, and Conversation Boost, may be more effective than ANC [noise-canceling headphones], which may block out the speaker's voice. These features improve audibility, reduce background noise, and focus on the person speaking in front, resulting in better speech intelligibility and listening comfort.

The technology we've described offers students with dyslexia wonderful options for improving classroom comfort and success.

Classroom Applications of Headphones

Many students and teachers learn to tune out the constant background noise that is part of any school. They easily sort sound into input they need to attend to and "static" they don't. However, some students, notably those with dyslexia, find the auditory environment of a classroom overwhelming due to their tendency to lose the signal in the background noise (Van Hirtum et al., 2021). This makes it exhausting to try to concentrate on classwork.

We marvel that some teachers don't want students using headphones. High school students are asked to do difficult mental work like mathematics, reading, or writing in congested spaces surrounded by other people. Many people who work in computer science, remote customer service, accounting, or many other fields routinely use headphones when they need to concentrate. It's reasonable to let students use the same tool.

Integrating headphones into your classroom will vary depending on you and your students' needs. We offer some suggestions you may want to try in the following sections.

Make Friends With Music

Surprisingly, some students who are extremely sensitive to environmental noise can concentrate while listening to music, even heavy metal. How is this possible? It makes sense when you consider that the music blocks out random noises that are hard to sort. The student may know the music well enough to put it into the background noise category. They don't have to constantly sort out what's happening or which sound to listen to. White noise or silence works better for others. Eddie, the mechanic we mentioned in the introduction (page 1), told us the following:

> When I study, I listen to rock music very loud. For some reason, this makes the reversal and disorientation settle down. I can do trig in my head when listening to loud music, but don't do so well on paper in classroom noise. (Eddie, personal communication, January 20, 2021)

Obviously, we don't recommend music so loud it damages hearing, but we want to acknowledge that different brains work best in different auditory environments.

You may be inspired by this list produced by National University (n.d.) of top music genres to listen to while studying.

- **Classical:** Classical music can be soothing and may increase productivity and elevate mood, all of which make it a good option for studying.

- **Spa music:** The kind of ambient sounds you might hear during a spa treatment may help you relax.

- **Nature sounds:** As with ambient music, the sounds of rain, birdsong, a running stream, or a gentle breeze make calming background noise. Websites like Noisli (www.noisli.com) let you create your own mix.

- **Electronic music:** New-age and even ambient electronic dance music (EDM) with few to no lyrics may be good choices if you don't like classical music.

- **Lofi hip-hop:** This type of hip-hop is lowkey, has fewer beats per minute (BPM), incorporates natural sounds, and frequently has no vocals, making it an unobtrusive choice for studying.

- **Jazz:** Listening to jazz may heighten creativity and reduce stress; mellow or chill jazz are optimal for concentration and study.

- **Ambient playlists:** Premade playlists with themes like "autumn bookstore coffee shop" featuring mellow jazz or "cozy cabin evening" with falling rain and crackling fireplace sounds can create the right mood for a productive study session.

- **Film or game soundtracks:** Selecting a favorite or familiar video game or movie soundtrack can help concentration. You can find compilations of film and game scores online.

Offer Headphones to All Students

The most powerful reading-improvement tool for students with dyslexia is tracking (chapter 3, page 73). Tracking along with the text while a computer or other reading device replicates a spoken voice lets learners with dyslexia experience high-level text in a way that works beautifully with dyslexic strengths. It consistently improves reading vocabulary and comprehension. Since we know that tracking helps students with dyslexia, and headphones are needed for the comfort of both the listener and those nearby, why would anyone want to argue against headphones for students with dyslexia or any other neurodiverse condition that headphones might benefit?

If a simple tool like headphones makes study happier and more productive for these students, shouldn't headphones be available to all students without the stigma of being a special accommodation?

Of course, you don't want students wearing headphones while you explain a new concept, unless you are lucky enough to have a teacher microphone wirelessly linked to the student headphones. You may therefore want to make a sign that says, "Headphones off, please." You can start tomorrow with the small change of permitting headphone use during individual work. This small shift may dramatically increase productivity for many students.

Students may have headphones that allow them to hear you when they turn off other input. However, we like to ask all our students to remove headphones during class instruction because then the rule is the same for everyone regardless of headphone type, and because it's good manners for the workplaces these students may soon enter.

To assist this shift to a headphone-friendly classroom, provide one or two sets of headphones for students to use.

Put some alcohol wipes next to the classroom headphones so students can clean them between uses. Just let the students know they are available and what they are for, then watch to see what happens.

Along with a few classroom headphones, allow students to bring their own headphones. Most students already own headphones or earbuds and only need your permission to use them.

Another small step involves taking a five-minute class poll. Tally how many students use headphones outside of class to aid concentration or to track along with a book. Find out who listens to music while they study and what kind of music they prefer. Find out how many like to study in silence or at the library. Marvel together at the glorious diversity of the human brain and make clear that all brains are wonderful. Encourage students to study in ways that fit their beautiful brains. Simply having this discussion gives students permission to experiment with different ways of increasing their own concentration and focus.

The following are some of the things we've heard from students about using headphones.

- "My headphones help me block out distractions and focus in class. It's hard for me to concentrate when I can hear everyone else talking and making noise."

- "I deal with anxiety, and listening to music through my headphones helps me calm down and feel more relaxed and focused during school."

- "Sometimes I need to listen to a concept a few times to really understand it. My headphones help me do that without distracting others."

- "My headphones let me create my own personal space. It's like having a little bubble where I can focus on my work without interruptions."

- "I struggle with filtering out background noise, so my headphones help me tune in to what the teacher is saying and tune out the other noise in the classroom."

Assuming you would like to offer your students the benefit of headphones, there are things they need to know. It's best to be clear about how students may use headphones responsibly and safely in your class. We've listed the information we feel is important to cover with high school students.

- Make sure the volume on your headphones is turned down low enough that you can still hear what's happening around you. You should be able to hear your teacher or classmates if they need to get your attention.

- The volume on your headphones should be set at no more than 50 to 60 percent of maximum volume, or between 40 and 75 dBA, if you are able to measure it. The longer you listen, the lower the volume should be.

- If you have a safe listening feature on your headphones or a smartphone app to monitor your sound exposure, please use it.

- Take five-minute breaks once per hour to let your ears rest.

- Remove your headphones when the teacher speaks to the class. Even if you can hear the teacher with your headphones on, removing them signals that you are listening.

- Be considerate of others and of your future hearing. Ask the person sitting next to you if they can hear your headphones. If they can, turn them down.

- Use comfortable headphones that fit well, if possible. This makes for more study and less fiddling. It also makes your study much more enjoyable.

- Invest in a good pair of headphones if you are able. Getting a quality pair of headphones will make a difference compared to the cheap earbuds included with most phones.

- Keep your headphones clean. Just give them a quick wipe-down every day.

- Label your headphones with your name and contact information. If they get lost, someone can quickly return them to you.

- Never loan out your personal headphones to anyone. This keeps them clean and handy.

This list is also available at **go.solutiontree.com/literacy** as a student-ready reproducible.

Save Teacher Time Too

If your school uses headphones that connect to the teacher's microphone, you have a captive audience. You can speak to your students without interruptions or background noise interfering. This saves you time because you don't need to repeat yourself. Additionally, the chance to use headphones may be rewarding to students, making them happier to settle down and get to work. This reduces your behavior management time. This effect may be most powerful with the more disruptive students.

How to Address Pushback From Naysayers

Hopefully, you will have no need to defend your classroom choices to anyone—but if you do, here are a few common concerns you may hear from other educators or student caregivers.

"If I let students use headphones, they will listen to music."

This is true, but it might not be bad. Working for thirty years with neurodiverse students taught us that some students flourish academically when allowed to choose an auditory environment. Some students prefer silence, some prefer white noise, and others prefer music. Some even prefer the complex background noise of a public space like a coffee shop. There are even students who thrive in a noisy classroom environment. Our brains differ in this regard, so permitting students to choose when possible makes sense.

Music allows some people to focus. It can calm anxiety. Music may raise mood and sense of well-being. Often, music or background sounds that the teacher finds helpful differ from what the student finds helpful. That's OK if the student is allowed headphones. We recommend high-quality, comfortable noise-canceling headphones if your school or the student can afford them, but even earbuds can provide welcome benefits.

"Headphones will damage students' hearing."

Hearing loss because of excessive noise levels is a common and reasonable concern. Of course, listening to loud sounds through headphones is harmful to hearing. However, noise levels at school can sometimes be high enough that headphones actually protect hearing when used correctly (Smith, 2021). The concern about hearing damage while using headphones is a primary reason we think it's worth a teacher's time to do a lesson on headphone usage, even if you don't end up using headphones in your class. Science or health teachers may want to slip in a minilesson on decibel levels, but for most of us it's sufficient to tell students that if their neighbor can hear their headphones, the volume is too high.

"How can I get their attention if they have headphones on?"

A visual signal that you need everyone's attention works well. This can be a sign, a flag, or a flashing light. Students may come up with even more creative ideas! Learning some sign language might be fun and can be used with new vocabulary words as well.

With this in mind, we spoke with Daniel Campbell, retired provost and biology professor at SouthWest College for the Deaf in Big Spring, Texas. At this school, flashing lights replace bells and other auditory signals. The school mascot is a rattlesnake with a light bulb at the end of its tail. We can all learn to attend to signals other than sound. Most students enjoy learning a bit of sign language, whether they have deaf friends or family or not. Using American Sign Language to ask students to remove headphones adds a bit of fun without adding noise.

"Where do I get all these headphones? I'm on a tight budget."

Unfortunately, this is real. If the school can't supply headphones or even earbuds for students, you may be forced to ask businesses or parent groups to donate. We wish teachers weren't put into this position, but we know it's common. However, most students now have their own earbuds at least, so your permission to use them may be all that's needed. You'll only need to find headphones or earbuds for a few students, not the whole class. Students may have extras that they are happy to donate to the class.

Summary

In this summary section, we offer a quick list of the main points covered in this chapter, followed by questions for reflection.

- Headphones come in a variety of forms; familiarity with the options helps teachers and students choose what works best in their classrooms.

- Headphones can help students with dyslexia by allowing them to use tracking for study and pleasure reading.

- People with dyslexia exhibit low ability to sort speech from background noise, so they may miss parts of discussions or lectures.

- Providing headphones or giving permission to use headphones immediately makes your classroom more dyslexia friendly while possibly satisfying 504 or IEP requirements at the same time.

- Headphones used correctly protect hearing rather than damage it.

- Listening to music while doing independent work may aid some students' concentration. For others, music can be a distraction.

- Headphone use in the classroom can reduce behavior management time for the teacher because the most disruptive students are often pleased to put on their headphones and get to work.

Reflection

Use the following questions to further consider this chapter's new tool and how you can use it to help struggling readers.

1. Does your school supply headphones? If not, do your students already have headphones or earbuds they can use in class as needed?

2. Have you allowed students to use headphones in class before? Do you, or would you, find the use of headphones in class to be helpful or distracting?

3. Do you think a short lesson on headphone usage for study would benefit your students, even if you don't employ this technology in class?

4. How might you address misuse of headphones in your classroom?

5. How might incorporating more headphone use in your classroom help your neurodiverse students?

Reproducible Forms With Suggested Standards and IEP and 504 Goals

Headphone use likely doesn't require a formal lesson plan, as this tool can be seamlessly introduced using the simple strategies provided in this chapter. Good luck in your explorations of this versatile tool!

CHAPTER 5

Implementing Recorded Lessons

**Luckily, the fundamental role of a teacher is not to deliver information.
It is to guide the student in the social process of learning . . .
The most important thing a teacher does
is make every student feel like they are important,
to make them feel accountable for doing the work of learning.**
—DEREK ALEXANDER MULLER

Michelle Russell (2024), a high school mathematics teacher, shares how recording herself while teaching helped her identify areas for improvement in her teaching as well as students who may need additional support. Her blog, Meaningful Math (http://middleweb.com/category/meaningful-math), is a great resource for teachers and educators to gain new ideas, and we highly recommend checking it out. Specifically, we would like to draw attention to the benefits of lesson recording, which Michelle highlights in her blog.

Michelle recorded herself teaching a class, and after watching the resulting video, was taken aback by what she saw.

> When I sat down to watch my first lesson, it was difficult. Reality turned out to be much different than the idea that I had in my head. However, after I got past the initial discomfort at watching myself, I could actually start noticing what was going on in my classroom. (Russell, 2024)

Michelle observed herself as she interacted with her students. She noticed that she sometimes interrupted students and answered questions herself. She also realized that she was spending more time with certain student groups than others. As she watched, she made short notes about what worked well and what she wanted to change.

Michelle realized these videos were key to improving her skill as a teacher. Recording yourself as you teach can be intimidating, but as Michelle so cogently communicates, it can open new avenues for professional development specific to your own situation.

But what does this have to do with dyslexia in the high school classroom? Recording technology now allows teachers to easily produce audio or video recordings that students can watch as needed to study, review, or catch up. This is especially helpful for students with dyslexia, as we'll show in the research section.

In this chapter, we will first explore the technology that allows teachers to record themselves teaching, then investigate the research on the effects of using recorded lessons in your classroom. Finally, we will share some ideas about how to use this technology effectively and in a way that supports students with dyslexia as well as saves you time.

What Recorded Lessons Are

Despite that fact that YouTube has thousands of teacher videos and many of them are excellent, we think short videos you make of yourself teaching can also be a wonderful tool that bolsters the ability of students with dyslexia to learn the material you have spent so much time preparing and presenting. By setting a phone, tablet, or computer on a desk at the front of the room and turning on video recording on the camera, you can make your presentation available for those who need to see it again and those who missed it.

You have something those YouTube videos cannot duplicate: a knowledge of your students' current understanding and a feel for the community and culture they live in. Most importantly, you have a relationship with these students. The videos you make are one more way to show you want all your students to understand the material and succeed in your class.

At one time, recording lessons was a cumbersome task. The technology was expensive and not user friendly. The results were often of poor video quality and audio clarity. Moreover, the recorded lessons were rarely shared with anyone other than the state education office that issued teacher certifications.

A lot has changed in the past few years. Now, with the help of technology, you can easily record your teaching sessions with your phone, tablet, or laptop. There are three basic approaches to recording a lesson.

1. Record yourself and your students while teaching your class. If you choose this option, remember to obtain permission from your students to be filmed.

2. Record only yourself teaching a live class.

3. Record yourself teaching a concept without a class.

Lesson recording is a tool that benefits students with dyslexia, as the research in the next section shows. If you're looking for classroom ideas rather than research, feel free to skip the research section and dive straight into the subsequent section, Classroom Applications of Recorded Lessons (page 133).

How Recorded Lessons Help Students With Dyslexia

Recording your lessons can help students with dyslexia by providing a way to replay and clarify directions and concepts. Kim Ramsey (2020), former K–12 educator and director of partner success at Boclips, which produces recording technology for classrooms, summarizes research from the University of Michigan and the British Dyslexia Association:

> It's important to provide accommodations for dyslexic learners so that resources are accessible and students feel involved in their learning. Video is a perfect tool for strategies such as combining visual and aural information. . . . Plus, videos come with a whole host of other features that can be beneficial for those with dyslexia. For example, captions can help students match words with pronunciations and the ability to rewind or pause a video gives learners an opportunity to review the content.

Ramsey's summary is right on target in our experience; recorded lessons are a boon for students with dyslexia.

For most neurotypical students, the physical act of taking notes improves focus and helps to imprint the information they are learning. However, for students with dyslexia, who may also experience dysgraphia (see page 52 in chapter 2), taking notes can be so difficult that it interferes with their ability to listen to and understand the lesson. Recording your lesson can ease that cognitive load (International Dyslexia Association, 2020b).

Most of the research we found on lesson recording has been done with university students, perhaps because it's much easier to obtain their permission and participation since they are usually age eighteen or older. We feel this research applies to high school students as well, since there is little age difference involved.

Education scholars Larian M. Nkomo and Ben Kei Daniel (2021) conducted research using detailed questionnaires to find out whether recorded lectures by professors affected learning outcomes for students and, if so, in what ways. A total of 660 students volunteered to participate in the survey, which took place at a public university in New Zealand. While these participants were university students, the classroom environments they describe are similar to high school classrooms in that they involve a combination of lectures, projects, and independent work and readings.

The project was part of institutional research to provide better strategies to support learning and teaching with digital learning technologies. The conclusion of Nkomo and Daniel's (2021) study strongly supports the use of lesson recording to make classroom content more flexible and convenient. They state the following:

> For over a decade, studies have shown that many higher education students are overwhelmingly advocating for lecturers to record their lectures and make them available.... The availability of lecture recordings assures students that they can catch up on their schoolwork if they miss lectures for any reason. Availability of these resources can help reduce student anxiety. (p. 27)

While Nkomo and Daniel (2021) did not separate dyslexic from neurotypical students, the overwhelmingly positive response to recorded lessons from the students in this study highlights how helpful this tool is for all students.

Educators have raised concerns that the wide-scale provision of lesson recordings to students is likely to have a detrimental effect on learning and that some students may choose to use these materials as a substitute for attending class. However, studies have also revealed that recordings offer students increased flexibility to access learning anywhere and anytime and have less influence on students' choices to attend class (Topale, 2016).

As mentioned above, Nkomo and Daniel (2021) find these positive results for all students, since they did not separate out the students with dyslexia in the study. However, they note that "recordings provided students with the ability to juggle multiple demands, and supported flexible access for students with medical conditions or learning disabilities" (p. 26). Your recorded lessons make your content more accessible to all students, especially those with dyslexia.

Having established that lesson recording may be a valuable tool for high school teachers and their students with dyslexia, we now move to specific types of recording devices.

Smart Pens

Most classroom recording produces a video that can become a class resource, as the teacher can post it on YouTube or the school website. However, one recording device is designed to be a personal note-taking assistant: the smart pen. We expect to see more of these in high school classrooms soon, since they are becoming popular in college classrooms (Frankenberger, n.d.).

Caryl Frankenberger (n.d.), in a blog post for the Yale Center for Dyslexia & Creativity, describes how a smart pen works. She shares that the pen can be used like any standard pen but includes a microphone and a camera aimed downward to look at specially dotted paper one can buy or print. This allows students to take only a minimum of notes—a keyword here or there—while the pen records the entire lesson. Later, the student can tap the pen on a word they wrote to replay the part of the lesson where they wrote down that word.

Frankenberger (n.d.) explains how the smart pen helps students with dyslexia:

> If you are a slow writer, have difficulty taking notes, or simply want to record the speaker, tap on the "record" icon at the bottom of the page and the pen will record what is said from that moment on. Stop the recording whenever you want by tapping on the "stop" or "pause" icon. If you choose to record and take notes simultaneously, you can spend more time listening to the speaker and then write only the most important information. Later on you can go back and listen to any part of the audio recording by tapping anywhere on your written notes. The audio will begin from that point in your notes. If when listening to the audio recording you discover you have missed important information, you can add it to your notes at that time.

It's easy to see how smart pen technology, which lets the student control the lesson recording, could allow students with dyslexia to succeed in the classroom.

There are few privacy concerns since the smart pen camera is pointed down at the paper. However, smart pen technology is still somewhat expensive and probably not something the school can provide. Even so, don't hesitate to contact the special education department in your school to see if there is any funding available. Another option is a smartphone, which most high school students already have.

Smartphones

Using a smartphone to take a photo of the board or of someone else's notes is a quick way to accommodate for not being able to write fast enough to take good notes. Students can also use smartphones to video record lessons. But is using a smartphone in the classroom a good idea? Let's hear from both teachers and students.

Megan E. Gath, Lauren Monk, Amy Scott, and Gail T. Gillon (2024) of the Child Well-being Research Institute, University of Canterbury, New Zealand, conducted a cross-sectional survey to determine perspectives on students' smartphone use in the classroom. Participants in this research included 217 educators and 332 students from schools across New Zealand. Educators came from eighty-nine different schools, largely representing secondary schools. Students ranged in age from seven to eighteen. Seventy percent of the students in the study were from secondary schools (Gath et al, 2024). Gath and colleagues (2024) conclude the following:

> This research provided insight into the views of both educators and students, regarding the access, regulation, and use of mobile phones at school. On balance, both the educators and students were in favour of the school-level regulation of student phone use, but they were less in favour of a total ban approach. Most participants thought that students should not be allowed to have phones during class time, with rationale that centred around student learning and safety. Taken together, this research provides guidance for schools and governments that are considering the use of mobile phone policies in schools and indicates that an 'all-or-nothing' approach may not be the best. (p. 16)

The respondents in the survey pointed out both benefits and downsides of phone use. The conversation is complicated.

As *Newsweek* reporter Aliss Higham (2024) points out, "The debate over phones in schools has been ongoing since they became a significant part of everyday life in the mid-2000s." Your school, your community, and your students present a unique set of challenges regarding cell phones in classrooms. Arguments for having students keep their cell phones include safety and parent contact in case of a shooting or storm incident, health-monitoring apps for diabetes or epilepsy, and the ability to research and fact check easily.

Obviously, these arguments are countered by the huge distraction factor that cell phones present. High school teachers face the real danger that students can use their phones to record them and use that footage to slander them by changing the audio track. Likewise, phones can easily be used to bully and harass.

Research can provide data, but the classroom teacher, in our opinion, is the one to make a decision on phone use in their classroom. This decision will necessarily be nuanced, based on numerous factors distinct to each teacher's situation. Whether you allow students to record your lessons on their cell phones, or record your lessons yourself on your phone, are decisions we think are yours to make in your classroom. Of course, if your school bans phones, you will need to use other technologies if you wish to try lesson recording.

Computers and Video Recording

Beyond smart pens and cell phones, there are dozens of devices that can record audio and video and are adaptable for classroom use. A laptop computer with a camera and microphone will do a decent job.

It's also now possible to wear a device that links to a swiveling camera and microphone that follow you around the room as you teach, recording the entire lesson, including students' responses (https://swivl.com). We'll explore the legal considerations of this in the classroom section.

We've seen research indicating that video recordings of lessons, with accompanying subtitles if possible, can be a great resource for all students, especially those with dyslexia. We've touched on devices for recording lessons and suggested that phones be carefully controlled due to legal privacy concerns. We will address privacy more a little later in the chapter, but first, let's explore some creative ways to use lesson recording in your classroom to enhance your effectiveness with your students, especially those with dyslexia.

Classroom Applications of Recorded Lessons

Some teachers will find recording themselves an excellent way to increase accessibility for their students with dyslexia. Other teachers may find this a burden they don't care to take on.

There should be no pressure to use this tool if it doesn't feel right for your classroom. However, current technologies such as smart pens, laptops, tablets, and smartphones make it easy to have a student you trust record your lessons as you teach, thus removing that task from your personal workload.

If all your lesson visuals are computer based, video players such as QuickTime Player enable you to turn on the recording, present the lesson in front of the computer, and save the recorded file to upload to any site. A media player is likely already on your computer; if not, look for it as a download from the internet.

A media player will record anything you do on the computer including videos, slide presentations, and so on. It will also record your voice while talking through the lesson. It's best to do the recording in a quiet room as it is surprising how sensitive the computer's microphone can be. Keeping the lessons (or chunks of lessons) to about five to six minutes each will make it easier for students to grasp the information and find specific lessons in a long list of videos. It is less stressful if you make a mistake and have to rerecord a five-minute video rather than a twenty-minute lesson. And it will take less time to upload the video files to websites.

The COVID-19 pandemic brought about some negative experiences for teachers in regard to lesson recording. Teachers were suddenly asked to manage remote classrooms with little or no training in the technology involved. Lessons had to be reworked nearly overnight. Many teachers found themselves working from home with family members and pets interrupting their attempts. We have tremendous respect for the heroic efforts of teachers during that time.

Now, it's time to move forward from those difficult and frustrating days and embrace the use of recording technology to simplify your work and provide excellent assistance to all your students, particularly those who are dyslexic. The bonus, as Russell (2024) related at the beginning of this chapter, is that you can watch the videos yourself to improve your delivery and interaction.

Recorded lessons benefit students with dyslexia as an easy way to review material while also saving time for the teacher. How does this work out in a classroom?

You can start lesson recording with baby steps. There's no need to become an overnight tech wizard. We urge you to give it a try, since the time investment can be small, and the payoff in student engagement and teacher time saved can be huge.

Lloyd Wafer (n.d.), a high school teacher and blogger, shares five ways lesson recording improves his teaching experience and saves him time. We've summarized his five points here, but the entire article is well worth reading when considering your own use of lesson recording as a teaching tool. The personal experiences he relates touch on challenges faced by most high school teachers.

The following are five ways lesson recording can help you save time (Wafer, n.d.)

1. **Recording is a powerful tool for self-reflection:** Teachers need to constantly refine their practice, yet we often teach in isolation without opportunities to observe other teachers. Lesson recording allows teachers to observe each other on our own schedules.

Recording your lessons builds a digital teaching portfolio for end-of-year performance review or National Board Certification, saving time you might have spent gathering materials.

2. **There's no need to reteach lessons for absent students:** Lesson recording provides ready-to-watch lessons that students can watch at their convenience, even from home. This may be the biggest time saver of all.

3. **Recording can serve as homework coaching for both parents and students:** Lesson recording means you don't need to explain your homework to multiple parents or students. One great example is a new mathematics technique that's radically different from the techniques most of your students' parents used. Rather than explaining the technique to each parent, you can send them a video of your classroom demonstration. Or you can post the video to your classroom Google Drive or website. Your students with dyslexia will love being able to pause and replay, and their parents will be grateful. This is a way teachers can work smarter, not harder. Homework-help videos can save you huge amounts of time.

4. **Recording is great for learning center introductions:** Setting your students up to use centers independently can be time consuming. But if you record a brief introductory video explaining a learning activity and then set up a laptop at the center with headphones, your students can simply watch the instructional video when they arrive at the center. This saves a lot of repetition and supports students with dyslexia who may need extra time to digest instructions.

5. **Recording improves classroom management:** Students behave better when they know they're being recorded. If you have permission to record your students, you may be surprised at how well everyone behaves when they know that others will be able to see the video.

Try to keep your videos under five minutes. If lessons are long and complicated, then chunk them into a series of five-minute videos. Make sure each video is clearly titled and numbered so students can find material they need easily. When you are concise and organized, it lowers confusion for all students, especially those with dyslexia, and invites students of all reading levels to participate in your class more easily. Everyone wins.

Get Permission Before You Record

Before recording a classroom session that will show students, you'll need to have permission from students and their parents or guardians to be filmed. If you plan to upload the video to a YouTube channel or school website, make that explicit in the permission form.

Any time a lesson recording is done in a live classroom, there is a possibility that students may be identifiable in the video by sight or name. If a video contains personally identifiable information about students, it is an education record protected under the Family Educational Rights and Privacy Act (FERPA), the federal student privacy law. Wise teachers stay on the safe side of this law. This is a great reason to restrict phone use in the classroom except under carefully prescribed conditions.

If the only person in the video is you, the teacher, there's no problem. If students' voices are heard but are not easily identifiable, that's fine. If, however, students are identifiable, you will need each student's parent or guardian to sign a release form allowing the use of their personally identifiable information. (If the student is over eighteen, the student may sign their own release.)

Many schools now include these releases as part of registration. If that's the case at your school, all you need to do is check student records to see if any of your students or their caregivers did not sign the release. Guidance on how to navigate this bit of classroom law is available in concise and easily accessed form through North Carolina University at Charlotte's webpage "Classroom Recordings and FERPA" (North Carolina University at Charlotte Office of Legal Affairs, n.d.). We've summarized the major concerns in this section, but we also recommend visiting the site for more detail if questions arise in the course of doing your recordings.

Consider including wording in your syllabus such as, "Class sessions may be audio- or video-recorded for the purposes of student reference and access by other students enrolled in the same course." This does not replace getting permission from each student, but it's best practice.

To summarize, if you are the only person who appears in the recording, there is no conflict with any part of FERPA. If students appear in the video, it can only be shown to those students, unless they have signed a form allowing their personal information to be shared.

Determine Whether Students Can Record on Their Own Devices

The difficulties that can arise from phones in classrooms lead us to favor teacher-made videos, or videos made by one student the teacher has chosen for that task, rather than a wide-open policy allowing all students to do their own phone recordings. Since there are multiple ways to record lessons, we hope teachers won't feel pressured to do it any certain way, but experiment to find a good fit.

When considering whether your particular classroom should allow phone use for lesson recording, these questions may help.

- Does your district have a policy on phone use in class? If so, you must follow that policy.

- Do you see a need for students to use their phones in class to record lessons, to take pictures of notes, or for other educational purposes? Do your students with dyslexia have other avenues for review such as teacher-recorded lessons?

- Would it be reasonable to allow a few minutes to take photos of notes at the end of the lesson?

- Would you prefer to provide prepared notes for students who want them?

- Are you aware of cyberbullying, parents texting students, off-task web browsing, or other inappropriate use of phones in your student population that would make phone use in your classroom more trouble than it's worth?

Use your teacher's intuition and make a decision that works for both you and your students.

Decide Where to Put Recordings

Short videos explaining key concepts are easy to make, require no permissions, and probably won't need much editing. They are easy to upload to your YouTube channel or another video platform that autogenerates subtitles. We suggest having someone guide you through the process the first time if you've not done it before. You will need to edit the subtitles, as they are never perfect. The editing process is easy, but once again, having a guide on the first attempt will save a lot of time. You probably have a student who can serve as that guide.

One of the best aspects of short concept videos is that those videos become part of your resources for future classes.

Jazz Up Your Productions

If you enjoy this teaching tool and you want videos that are more sophisticated than just talking to your phone, Edpuzzle.com or Descript.com, among many others, can be a huge help.

EdPuzzle is a web-based tool that allows teachers to create video lessons by embedding questions, voiceovers, and other interactive content into videos. Descript is an online video-editing tool that allows you to generate audio based on text. You can also create an AI clone of your voice and add or change audio by typing. You can edit audio and video like you would edit a document. You can cut, copy, and paste, and use templates and layouts.

Watching other teachers' videos is top-notch professional development. You'll likely see techniques and ideas you'd like to try as well as pick up hints about how to make an effective video recording. Please don't be intimidated by those who seem ridiculously adept at videography. Your students will connect more with your first attempts than they will with a professional video, because they know you and can tell you are trying to make learning easier for them.

Save Teacher Time Too

We've already touched on saving time earlier in the chapter. Now we want to add detail to this important aspect of lesson recording. Your time is precious.

Lesson recording can save teachers time since they won't have to repeat themselves. For example, teachers can answer questions once and record the answers rather than explaining multiple times to different students. Teachers can also arrange synchronous online sessions where students can ask questions. Recordings of these sessions can be uploaded to a lesson-capture platform for students to access at their convenience.

The most important time-saving aspect of recorded lessons is the library of material you will build that you can use repeatedly.

How to Address Pushback From Naysayers

Hopefully, you will have no need to defend your classroom choices to anyone—but if you do, here are a few common concerns you may hear from other educators or student caregivers.

"Won't I get in trouble if I record copyrighted material, such as reading from a textbook in a recorded lesson?"

Teachers have special privileges regarding copyright laws. Here's a summary from attorney Rich Stim (n.d.):

> Fortunately, the Copyright Act contains a special exception for educational uses of copyrighted materials. Under what is known as the "fair use" rule, someone other than the copyright owner may make limited use of a copyrighted work without permission for purposes such as teaching, research, scholarship, criticism, parody and news reporting.

"I don't like seeing myself on camera."

Understandably, we aren't all part of the selfie generation. It can be intimidating at first to post a video of yourself teaching, since students and other teachers, not to mention administration, can see it and make judgments about it.

Let us suggest that you start with short audio recordings with the camera pointing at anything you use to illustrate your lessons, even a textbook page or photos related to what you are explaining. You can write on the whiteboard and aim the camera at the board. You can draw cartoons illustrating your point and aim the camera at the paper. We hope you will start trying things, even if it feels uncomfortable. But we recommend starting slowly, with just one or two videos.

If this still feels uncomfortable, we have another idea. The internet is full of great videos by wonderful teachers. You may find especially valuable videos to share with your students. You can watch them together and discuss. Give your students the link to the video so they can rewatch as needed or desired. Now you've offered them the advantage of video instruction they can refer to, and you've also discussed the material together, providing the teacher connection that's so important. This is a much richer and better learning experience than telling them to watch the video at home and take a quiz on it tomorrow. The focus has changed from trying to get the answers to the quiz to developing a deeper understanding through discussion and questions.

"Making videos takes time, and I already work way too many hours."

Making videos does take time, but once they are made and saved to your computer or YouTube channel, they can save you time. You can use them again and again, whenever you teach the same material. We've found that asking students to watch a video and report back to class with any questions they have can increase engagement among students who would normally try to get out of doing standard written homework. Thus, you can save time, honor the diverse learning styles of your students, and start great class discussions about real questions students have after watching the video.

"If I have students watch videos instead of do written homework, my class won't be seen as rigorous or worthwhile."

We aren't suggesting that you ditch all writing assignments. In fact, chapter 2 (page 49) shows ways of making writing assignments accessible for your students with dyslexia. Instead, we suggest introducing your own short videos about key concepts, then assess the effect on learning.

"My students spend too much time on YouTube already. If I post videos there, they'll just get distracted."

YouTube isn't the only game in town. You can also post videos on your school website if it is set up for this. You may prefer Google Classroom or Canva for Education, two programs many schools use. Posting to a school-based site can help students stay focused with fewer distractions.

Summary

In this summary section, we offer a quick list of the main points covered in this chapter, followed by questions for reflection. Then, we introduce a list of IEP and 504 goals that are easily met using the tool of lesson recording.

- *Lesson recording* refers to using any device that records both audio and video to capture yourself teaching a class or explaining a concept.

- Research supports lesson recording because it allows students to pause, replay, study for a test, and bypass note-taking.

- Subtitles added to recorded videos boost reading vocabulary as students track along the text while listening (see chapter 3, page 73).

- Although lesson recording can seem intimidating or like an extra chore in your crowded day, ultimately it will save you time while making your classroom far more dyslexia friendly.

Reflection

Use the following questions to further consider this chapter's new tool and how you can use it to help struggling readers.

1. How do you feel personally about lesson recording?

2. Have you done any lesson recording for your classroom? What was that experience like?

3. How does lesson recording in the classroom differ from the lesson recording teachers were required to do during the pandemic?

4. Do you, or do you think you would, prefer recording alone with just the camera, or do you like the energy of recording student questions and discussions?

5. Would you consider collaborating with a student videographer? What might be the benefits or potential issues with this?

Reproducible Forms With Suggested Standards and IEP and 504 Goals

We adapted the reproducible list "Common IEP and 504 Goals That Lesson Recording May Meet" from a master list at Undivided (2025), a company providing support for students with disabilities and developmental delays. IEP goals may be stated in various ways; there's no magic in the phrases used here. We provide this list so you can quickly compare these common goals to goals that students in your classes have in their IEPs or 504s. It's helpful to know that video recordings of your lessons may meet multiple goals without adding any other tasks to your day. Additionally, if you need to provide evidence of compliance with the goals, your videos are readily available.

Common IEP and 504 Goals That Lesson Recording May Meet

Learning Environment
- Reduce visual distractions.
- Provide a clear view of the board, teacher, or screen.
- Allow for small-group or individual administration.
- Allow the use of assistive technology.

Curriculum and Directions
- Use both oral and printed directions.
- Give directions in small steps using as few words as possible.
- Provide visual aids.
- Record directions.
- Clarify, simplify, or repeat directions.

Textbooks
- Provide a summary of each chapter.
- Read questions or passages aloud.
- Provide written materials in alternate formats.
- Explore the use of assistive technology.
- Provide audio forms of textbooks; have students follow the text while listening.

Mathematics
- Read and explain story problems or break problems into smaller steps.
- Use pictures or graphics.

Test Taking and Grading
- Provide prerecorded audio delivery for assessments.

Behavioral Accommodation
- Arrange for the student to leave the classroom or learning area voluntarily and go to a designated safe place when under high stress. This could mean access to a computer and headphones to watch class-relevant videos.

Visual Processing
- Provide all materials in enlarged font.
- Provide video notes, handouts, or texts.

Auditory Processing
- Reduce background noise.
- Provide additional written or visual material.
- Simplify directions and verbal instruction.

page 1 of 2

Never Too Late © 2025 Solution Tree Press • SolutionTree.com
Visit **go.SolutionTree.com/literacy** to download this free reproducible.

Assignments

- Substitute alternatives for long writing assignments (such as clay models, posters, panoramas, collections, electronic presentations, oral presentations, or watching a video and discussing).
- Give alternatives to long written reports (for example, write several short reports, view audio-visual materials and write a short review, or give an oral report on an assigned topic).
- Shorten assignments to focus on mastery of key concepts.

Additional IEP or 504 Accommodations

- Introduce an overview of long-term assignments.
- Break long-term assignments into small, sequential steps.
- Structure work so that the easiest parts come first.

Source: Undivided. (2024, April 3). List of accommodations for IEPs and 504s. Accessed at https://undivided.io/resources/list-of-accommodations-for-ieps-and-504s-210 on May 20, 2024.

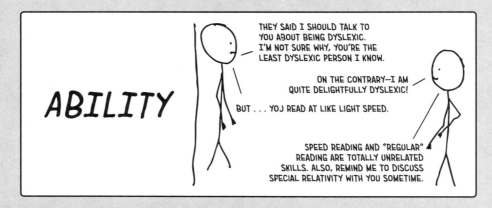
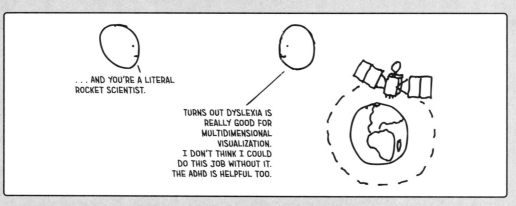
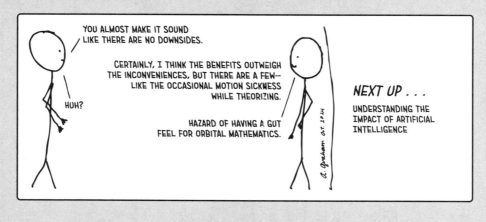

CHAPTER 6

Understanding the Impact of Artificial Intelligence

Teaching is probably the most difficult of all current jobs for an AI to manage. If you don't believe that, then you have never truly taught.
—HANK GREEN

Ilya Venger (2024) is a data and AI product lead at Microsoft. His blog article, "How a Bunch of High Schoolers Surprised Me With Their Take on AI," resonates strongly with us as high school teachers. We've shortened his story, but these are his words.

Venger (2024) writes that a friend invited him to talk with students participating in an extracurricular course on Greek mythology. The class Venger joined was about Pandora's box and how Pandora's curiosity led to her opening the box and unleashing evil on the world. He was struck by the analogy between the myth and the potential risks and promises of AI. Venger was also struck by the words of a shy fifteen-year-old girl in the class: "I tried ChatGPT," she said, explaining, "it can do a lot of things much better than I can—even if I learn hard. If the systems become even smarter, and can do anything I can do better . . . then what am I here for?"

Venger (2024) sees this as evidence that the students "showed an intuitive grasp of elements of existential risks" with AI. Citing a statement from Bill Gates, who said that his concern about AI "is human purpose," Venger observes, "The worries of a sixty-plus-year-old visionary tech billionaire and the anxieties of a bright, yet random, fifteen-year-old are the same." The experience prompted Venger (2024) to conclude the following:

> I don't fully understand the world, and I have my own (additional) worries about an AI-driven future. However, this cross-sectional and intergenerational echoing of concerns about human purpose voiced by tech leaders, intellectuals and youngsters makes the problem stand out for me now more than ever before.

Some of us are concerned and wish we could hold back these changes. Some of us are eager to see what the future holds. All of us care about the welfare of our students, our profession, and ourselves. As AI unfolds, we may all be asking, "What are we here for?"

High school teachers and their students with dyslexia may be the most important people on the planet as we plunge into the wild new world of AI. Why? Because high school teachers are in a unique position to help students wrestle with the questions raised by AI. High school teachers empower students to think and create, while dyslexic thinking may hold a key to living well with the machines we've made.

In this chapter, we show why we think AI holds promise as a wonderful tool for students with dyslexia, and also why students with dyslexia and their teachers may be the key to using AI well.

As an experiment, we initially wrote this chapter with assistance from Google AI Studio (https://aistudio.google.com) and from Google Assistant (https://assistant.google.com). *Assistance* is a key word in the last sentence. We prompted the AI to find up-to-the-minute research but followed the trail of that content to review the actual research written by real scientists, educators, and engineers. We asked the AI to provide a list of new vocabulary pertaining to AI in education, but then we read directly from experts in the field and composed simplified definitions and examples for the vocabulary we chose to list.

We even prompted the AI to write sections of the chapter based on our headings and questions, but we soon found that the resulting paragraphs were not what we wanted to say and added no value to the conversation, so we threw them all out. This is why you don't see citations for AI in this chapter. In short, we found AI assistance great for initial information gathering and for locating recent research but decidedly unhelpful for writing the chapter or guiding teachers through the changes that AI brings.

Despite our experience in writing this chapter, AI may turn out to be the most powerful educational tech tool ever invented, and it's evolving rapidly as we write. Students with dyslexia are already making use of AI-powered tutors at Khanmigo (n.d.) with impressive results that we'll detail later.

Let's explore what we can do to prepare students and teachers for this new phase of human history and its implications for struggling readers.

What Artificial Intelligence Is

AI is a field of computer science concerned with building programs that can learn by self-correcting using large amounts of data. These computer systems perform tasks that usually require human intelligence, like learning, communicating, problem solving, pattern finding, and decision making.

In most cases, when educators speak about AI they are talking about *generative AI*, which "refers to deep-learning models that can generate high-quality text, images, and other content based on the data they were trained on" (Martineau, 2023). That's not the same as artificial general intelligence, which hasn't quite happened yet. Tim Mucci and Cole Stryker (2024) at IBM provide a peek at our possible future with artificial general intelligence:

> Imagine a world where machines aren't confined to pre-programmed tasks but operate with human-like autonomy and competence. A world where computer minds pilot self-driving cars, delve into complex scientific research, provide personalized customer service and even explore the unknown. This is the potential of artificial general intelligence (AGI), a hypothetical technology that may be poised to revolutionize nearly every aspect of human life and work.

Right now, teachers work in a world of rapidly advancing generative AI. At the same time, both teachers and students wrestle with the probable entrance of AGI and what that means for culture in general and education in particular. High school teachers have a lot of practice walking this sort of path with each new technological breakthrough, so we have no doubt that just as teachers helped students adapt to computers, they will now lead the way in adapting to AI.

In education, AI comes in various forms, from intelligent tutoring systems adapted for individual students to voice-recognition software that assists with writing. AI programs can write tests and grade them. AI can plan lessons from brief prompts or format teacher feedback for parents and administrators. It writes stories, essays, and research papers (but be sure to check both facts and citations). It can translate into many languages, including American Sign Language via a signing avatar on video.

Of course, AI does none of these tasks with the integrity, creativity, nuance, or individuality of a teacher. AI is also prone to what some call *hallucinations*, providing entirely made-up ideas, content, and resources as if they were established facts (MIT Management, n.d.).

However, AI programs, by definition, are learning and becoming better all the time. We think these tools will revolutionize education. Nevertheless, this revolution does not mean AI can replace teachers because, despite unproven claims of AI sentience, AI is only a complex compilation of human language and images. It cannot care about a student.

What does AI mean right now for teachers and students with dyslexia? High school teachers have long been tasked with helping students sort facts from opinions in whatever field they teach. But now that's harder to do and requires some knowledge of what AI is capable of producing. No longer can we assume that if we see a photograph or video of an event, it actually occurred. Just because a paper looks like research and has citations doesn't mean it refers to actual research. Just because something sounds like a newscast doesn't mean it is reporting real news. Teachers will be at the forefront of helping students determine what to trust in this strange new landscape.

It also means that students with dyslexia have life-changing technology at their fingertips. They need teachers to guide them in how to use it wisely. To help with that task, we start with vocabulary.

The Vocabulary of AI

AI generates not only text, pictures, and cat videos, but also a great deal of new vocabulary, which can make reading, research, and keeping abreast of developments challenging. In our experience, this new vocabulary, which often includes unfamiliar acronyms or old vocabulary used in new ways, is one of the biggest barriers to understanding AI technology. With that in mind, we provide a quick look at terms you may need to know.

Following are some AI-related definitions that are relevant to educators.

- **Adaptive learning:** Adaptive learning is educational technology that uses AI to adjust the difficulty and pace of learning based on a student's individual needs and performance. Examples include sophisticated software such as Khan Academy and Duolingo since they adjust the difficulty of questions and amount of repetition based on student responses. Deborah L. Taylor, Michelle Yeung, and A. Z. Bashet (2021) define *adaptive learning platforms* as those that "provide students a flexible learning environment that can accelerate learning by creating an individualized learning path directed by prior knowledge and continuous assessment of performance" (p. 20).

- **Algorithm:** These are a set of instructions or rules that guide an AI system in processing information and making decisions (Khan, 2024).

- **Artificial general intelligence (AGI):** AGI means artificial intelligence that matches (or outmatches) humans on a range of tasks by taking in not only stored data, but also real-time data such as visual images from cameras, sounds from microphones, even smells and tactile information, and interpreting all this input in a human kind of way, albeit with more information than any human could have (Heaven, 2023).

- **Generative pretrained transformers (GPT):** These are computer-based networks that power AI applications such as ChatGPT. They allow apps to create human-like text and content such as music, text, and images. They also enable apps to answer questions in a conversational manner (Amazon Web Services, n.d.).

- **Hallucinations:** IBM (2023) defines AI *hallucination* as a "phenomenon wherein a large language model (LLM)—often a generative AI chatbot or computer vision tool—perceives patterns or objects that are nonexistent . . . creating outputs that are nonsensical or altogether inaccurate."

- **Jill Watson:** This is not a person—it's a groundbreaking AI-enabled virtual teaching assistant introduced at the Georgia Institute of Technology in 2016. Georgia Tech faculty Ashok Goel, David Joyner, and Spencer Rugaber (n.d.) recall the following:

> Jill answered only routine, frequently answered questions on the forum, but she did so with higher than ninety percent accuracy and with an authenticity that the students in the class did not figure out that Jill was actually an AI agent.

- **Large language model (LLM):** Northwood Tech Innovative Teaching and Learning Center (n.d.) clearly defines LLM as follows:

  > A Large Language Model (LLM) is a type of artificial intelligence that has been trained on a massive dataset of text and code. This allows them to generate text, translate languages, write different kinds of creative content, and answer your questions in an informative way.... Examples include ChatGPT, Gemini, Copilot, Claude, and Consensus.

- **Neural interface (NI), or brain-machine interface (BMI):** This is a computer device that interacts with the brain or nervous system of an individual and can be placed inside or outside the brain or body to record or stimulate activity. It can also replace, alter, or enhance impaired nervous system processes, such as in people with epilepsy or Parkinson's. It may allow paralyzed people to communicate with a computer using their thoughts. Neuroscientist and neuroengineer Krishna Shenoy (Stanford Alumni, 2021) directed the Stanford Neural Prosthetic Systems Lab, which helps restore lost motor function to people with paralysis. He explains how these devices work in a fascinating YouTube video, "Emerging Brain Computer Interfaces with Krishna Shenoy" (Stanford Alumni, 2021). Why do teachers need to know this? Because in the future you may have students who communicate via this technology.

- **Transformer:** Rick Merritt (2022), writing for Nvidia, explains, "A transformer model is a neural network that learns context and thus meaning by tracking relationships." This means that a transformer analyzes language by comparing and contrasting usage.

How Artificial Intelligence Helps Students With Dyslexia

Now that we have covered the vocabulary, we are ready to explore what AI does well and how teachers can use AI to improve learning outcomes for students with dyslexia. Some researchers are already providing data in this field, so we'll look at their work along with reports from high school teachers who are using AI in their classrooms.

Since we are not computer scientists, we started our research by speaking with Max Planck, senior technical director and senior system engineer researcher at the Institute for Complex Additive Systems Analysis (ICASA). ICASA is the research division of New Mexico Tech that focuses on solving homeland security and national issues. Max's work involves big data and complex computer systems. Max was kind enough to provide this explanation:

> When an AI produces text, it is simply predicting the next word or phrase based on the series of words that came before. It calculates from its massive exposure to language what word has the highest percentage probability of being the next word. AI is just math. (M. Planck, personal communication, May 23, 2024)

So, when you are trying to get information out of a chatbot, word prediction is what's happening. You may get good information because the chatbot may have been trained on previous customer questions and answers.

You may also get nonsense, especially if your question is unusual. In the most basic sense, this is why AIs hallucinate. They don't explicitly understand the questions or answers they receive so much as they play an infinitely advanced game of word prediction that is still prone to error if the data it's trained on is insufficient.

We asked Max if he thinks AI will replace teachers. He feels that AI could provide low-level instruction as an adjunct to teaching and could equalize access to information but could never replace a skilled teacher (M. Planck, personal communication, May 23, 2024).

Salman Khan (2024), who invented Khan Academy, explains that AI tutors must be trained on massive amounts of expert teacher exchanges with students and then prompted to interact in a Socratic style with leading questions rather than answers. Sometimes, students prefer AI since it doesn't get impatient or judgmental. But AI can't relate to a student, even if it sounds like it can. For that, we need real teachers.

Education Week staff writer Lauraine Langreo (2024) shares that "Artificial intelligence experts have touted the technology's potential to transform K–12 into a more personalized learning experience for students, as well as for teachers through personalized professional development opportunities." As Khan (2024) points out, individualized education for every student is the Holy Grail of education. Before AI, this required one-on-one tutoring and therefore existed only for those who could afford it. This has made it difficult for many students with dyslexia to access the individualized instruction they need to read well, thus arriving in high school without the needed skills. With the arrival of AI tutors, individualized instruction for every student becomes possible.

Computer science scholar Andrea Zingoni and colleagues (2021) carried out a research project with seven hundred university students with dyslexia. The researchers employed experimental AI instruction using a program developed specifically to help students with dyslexia. Zingoni and colleagues (2021) explain the parameters of their study as follows:

> The core of the project is BESPECIAL, a software platform based on artificial intelligence and virtual reality that is capable of understanding the main issues experienced by students with dyslexia and to provide them with ad hoc digital support methodologies in order to ease the difficulties they face in their academic studies.

This software isn't commercially available yet, but it lets us see how AI may soon assist students with dyslexia. Zingoni and colleagues (2021) feel that quality dyslexia assistance using AI will happen, but at the time we're writing this book, the programs are still learning and do not provide reliable help.

While we don't advocate teaching to tests, we realize that high school students sometimes ask their teachers for help in raising their SAT or ACT scores. Students with dyslexia may test poorly due to misreading questions and language processing difficulties associated with dyslexia (Eide & Eide, 2023). AI may prove especially helpful for students who want to invest time and effort to attain better scores. Heather M. Ross (n.d.), reporting in *Washington FAMILY*, provides one example: "Dysolve AI is a program capable of helping people with dyslexia by mapping their areas of difficulty and designing tailor-made games to retrain the brain in the area the person finds challenging."

Ross (n.d.) reports that Dysolve's cofounder, Coral Hoh, saw students go from the tenth percentile in state testing to above the fiftieth percentile in one school year. These are impressive numbers if test success is the goal. Since test scores can be problematic for students with dyslexia, this is one way AI may prove useful. However, AI may make high-stakes testing unnecessary by providing performance data in other ways.

Josh Clark, head of Landmark School and chair of the International Dyslexia Association, explains that AI is at the stage of thoughtful experimentation for educators (Landmark School, 2023). He suggests trying various tools with students with dyslexia while listening to their experiences and staying involved in their learning process.

Clark thinks AI will be a useful tool for students with dyslexia because AI tutors can summarize a text or rewrite it at a lower vocabulary level. He foresees many more ways students with dyslexia may be able to use AI in the future and urges teachers to experiment along with their students (Landmark School, 2023).

Naturally, AI research into education, especially dyslexia education, has barely begun. The next few years will hopefully be rich in insights into how we use this powerful tool to the best advantage for ourselves and our students.

Classroom Applications of Artificial Intelligence

In this section, we present ideas for experimenting with AI in high school classrooms, with special attention to supporting students with dyslexia.

Matt Higgs is the vice president of global partnerships of Made by Dyslexia. As Higgs states, "From engineering, to marketing, to AI computing, the most commonly needed skill is complex problem-solving. Dyslexics have this in abundance. Put simply, dyslexics have the most sought-after skills in the world" (Made by Dyslexia, 2024, p. 31).

AI is a powerful tool, becoming more so every day. But AI cannot think new thoughts. It uses human thoughts garnered from stunningly large data sets to predict and collate in new ways. Dyslexic thinking could provide the piece that's missing from AI thinking.

When ChatGPT was released in 2022, it caused instant concern in education because AI, at its best, can write a better essay than many students, and it can do so in a few seconds. AI can do mathematics homework or fill in a worksheet. Fears of plagiarism and cheating rose (Khan, 2024). The following sections explore how we as high school teachers should respond.

Embrace and Teach Rather Than Ban

Early education responses to ChatGPT included AI detection technology, which is deeply flawed, expensive, and must be updated constantly to work at all. This technology compares a student paper scanned into a computer program with examples of AI writing and student writing. It didn't work well. Some school districts banned the use of AI, with questionable success (Khan, 2024).

We argue that for high school teachers and their students, with dyslexia or not, the answer to AI is not to ban but to adapt and embrace. This technology is not going away, so education at all levels must develop new approaches or become increasingly irrelevant.

While schools and districts look to systemic solutions and best practices to this challenge, we suggest that teachers ask the simple question, What value can AI offer my students? One resource to watch is Khan Academy, which provides interactive individual learning paths in mathematics, science, reading, computing, history, art history, economics, financial literacy, SAT, MCAT, and more. It also reports progress data on each student to teachers. It is free for anyone (Khan, 2024).

As ChatGPT was in development, Khan worked with OpenAI to build Khanmigo (https://khanmigo.ai), which is an AI-powered tutor. Khanmigo is designed to support deep student learning through Socratic questioning while reducing paperwork for teachers. For teachers, what normally takes hours of teacher time can be done quickly with Khanmigo: lesson differentiation, lesson plans, quiz questions, student groupings, hooks, exit tickets, rubrics, and more (Khanmigo, n.d.).

Although Khanmigo isn't marketed as a dyslexia tool, the individual pacing and ability to ask the tutor questions and get conversational answers modeled on great teachers make it an excellent dyslexia resource. The best way to find out if Khanmigo offers something you or your students want is to experiment with it yourself, especially as it continues to evolve.

The same holds true of other AI tools you might encounter. None are perfect, but it's worth being aware of what is available and how specific features of these tools might better support learning for your students with and without dyslexia alike.

Teach AI Literacy

To prepare students for the world that's coming, we need to teach and model AI literacy across every subject area. As teachers, we must not only embrace the future our students will live in but also communicate with parents and administration how critical AI literacy is for students.

AI literacy includes understanding how AI works and being fully aware that it isn't omniscient. It makes mistakes because it only knows what it's been told. AI programs are trained on human input: books, conversations, social media, videos, and so on. This material almost always contains some sort of bias or assumptions. Our students need to become experts at spotting bias and outright fakes.

Our message to students with dyslexia: Use AI, but never trust it. It's tempting, if written work is difficult, to assume the AI knows best, but that's simply not the case. Teachers can best encourage their students with dyslexia by reminding them of their ability to see the big picture and notice patterns (Eide & Eide, 2023). Using this ability is key to using AI as a tool, not a crutch.

When working with students, especially those with dyslexia, one technique we've found helpful is to compare AI responses to the verifiable information you are teaching. Comparing and contrasting the AI responses with the verified information embeds the material you are teaching while improving students' understanding of AI at the same time. It also helps build the essential vocabulary in your field that students with dyslexia may be missing.

As part of this discussion with students, we talk about what AI does well (information gathering) and what it does poorly (creativity and reflection on meaning). For example, so far, AI is horrible at humanities. It can write music in any style, but it will be boring if you listen for more than a few minutes. AI can deliver accurate historical information if prompted carefully, but it can't discuss the nuances of civil rights or what that means for your community. In these discussions, our students with dyslexia often shine, giving them added status among their peers.

Plan Your Lessons Assuming Students Will Use AI

AI, as we've detailed throughout this chapter, invites a lot of questions among educators. For example, What if students say they used voice typing but instead used AI-generated writing? What if students solved these mathematics problems using AI without applying any of their own understanding to the processes and concepts they need to learn? These misuses of AI are particularly tempting for students with dyslexia because they struggle so hard to keep up with high school–level reading and writing. Additionally, they often have advanced technical skills (Eide & Eide, 2023), making this pathway even more alluring.

AI-generated homework calls for radical rethinking by teachers. This rethinking needs to happen anyway. If you're concerned that students might cheat on homework to get a grade, ask yourself if grading homework is even necessary. Well before AI became a factor, many expert educators already made the argument that homework should be treated as ungraded practice (Townsley & Wear, 2020).

To avoid the problem of AI doing the homework, consider implementing homework in the form of short video lessons for students to watch along with a brief practice exercise so they know what questions to ask in class the next day. Then, use class time to provide guided practice that you, their trusted teacher, can ensure they understand. This sort of flipped classroom (Goodacre, 2018) allows students with dyslexia to take in material using their verbal strength, then ask questions in class, all while building reading vocabulary by turning on the captions on the videos.

If you need to grade for your school, then a short in-class quiz, with the option to retake, is a workable solution and doesn't trigger dyslexic test anxiety like a long, high-stakes test.

Accept What You Don't Know

No one will know everything about AI education. We certainly don't. It's far too complex and expanding rapidly. You'll notice that this classroom applications section doesn't offer many specific things to *do* with AI. That's because it's new, and the capabilities of AI are changing so fast that any techniques we might suggest would surely be outdated before you ever read this.

Instead, use your education and experience to evaluate which tools are helpful for your particular students as you encounter them. As part of this, observe how your students make use of AI and ask them questions about what works best for them. Do this especially with your students identified as dyslexic, as they and their families will be as motivated as anyone to know how new AI tools and features can support them.

Using these tools requires teachers and students to try new things and talk about the results, which Khan (2024) calls "educated bravery" (p. xxxii). Part of educated bravery is trusting our students to try things and processing the results with them. That's what makes a great high school teacher, and it's more important than all the cool technology that's ahead.

We think students with dyslexia will lead the way in adopting AI assistance with their studies as they use it to do the following.

- Improve reading fluency and comprehension
- Enhance writing skills
- Boost organization and time management
- Individualize learning paths
- Develop independence and confidence

High school teachers who understand the value of AI tools for students with dyslexia and encourage them to try them will make this transition easier and happier. Teachers and students both win.

Save Teacher Time Too

You don't need to jump into AI all at once. In fact, AI will silently creep into everything we do with or without our approval. AI will be on your phone, your word processor, websites, and anything you do on a computer. You might as well use it to save time.

AI can automate repetitive tasks. For example, you could use AI to grade multiple-choice quizzes, write lesson plans, generate personalized feedback, and create differentiated learning materials.

AI may assist communication by translating material for parents and guardians who speak different languages. Before you send out a parent letter in another language, be sure to have a native speaker edit it. AI can produce some funny and embarrassing translations, such as "a history of the George Shrub presidency" instead of George Bush. If you don't speak the language in question, you won't catch these until it is too late.

As students become adept at using AI tutors for basic information and skill work, you may have time to engage in more critical thinking, logic, and meaningful conversation with your students. That's probably the best part of your job, and AI may allow you to do more of that and less paperwork.

How to Address Pushback From Naysayers

Hopefully, you will have no need to defend your classroom choices to anyone—but if you do, here are a few common concerns you may hear from other educators or student caregivers.

"AI will replace teachers, and that's not good for students or teachers."

AI is a tool to augment teaching, not replace it. Teachers remain crucial for seeing the big picture of what information students need, guiding them toward the appropriate individualized instruction, providing emotional support, and fostering a positive and exciting learning environment.

"Technology is distracting and overwhelming. It's best to just ignore it."

Technology, and especially AI, can certainly be both distracting and overwhelming, as well as annoying. So we favor approaching AI with care while helping your students to understand what it can and cannot do. Certain aspects of AI may be extremely helpful for individual students, especially those with dyslexia, so we suggest experimenting with a few programs that meet specific needs.

"These tools are expensive!"

AI will be part of all new phones, tablets, and computers, so if your students use any of these, they will have access to AI in some form. In the United States, access to a computer or phone is so foundational that social assistance provides a phone before housing or jobs. This is because you have to have a phone to apply for housing and jobs. So most high school students will have at least some access to AI via their phone.

"How should I cite AI-generated material if I use it? And what should I teach my students about AI citation?"

If you use AI simply to learn information, you don't need to cite. You do, however, need to check the information for accuracy. If you quote AI-generated text such as a lesson plan, or use pictures, video, or music generated by AI, then academic honesty requires citation. Dalhousie University Libraries (n.d.) provides a handy citation guide, which recommends "crediting the author of the algorithm with a reference list entry and the corresponding in-text citation." The following are some examples of what AI citations may look like.

- **In-text citations:** The general rule for citing sources in text is (algorithm author, year).
    - Example of parenthetical citation in text: (OpenAI, 2023)
    - Example of narrative citation in text: OpenAI (2023)

- **Reference list:** To cite AI-generated content in bibliographies, reference lists, or footnotes, use the following style model.

  - OpenAI. (2023). ChatGPT (March 14 version) [Large language model]. https://chat.openai.com/chat. (Dalhousie University Libraries, n.d.).

We expect details of AI citation to evolve. The important idea is to credit the person or team who programmed and trained the AI and be transparent about where you got the information. As AI becomes ubiquitous, it may be impossible to know the algorithm author or date of release. We will all be in new territory here and will need to cite as much needed information as we can reasonably get.

We expect there will soon be AI tools developed to track information and generate appropriate citations. That's not the case yet. In fact, current AI algorithms commonly generate citations of books and articles that don't exist. The AI isn't "lying," it's just a mathematical algorithm predicting a probability based on the information it has.

Summary

In this summary section, we offer a quick list of the main points covered in this chapter, followed by questions for reflection. Finally, we provide a list of IEP and 504 accommodations that AI may help meet.

- AI programs are revolutionizing our world, including education, at an astounding pace.

- Teachers won't choose whether or not to interact with AI; rather, AI will be part of everything we do on a computer or phone.

- High school teachers can assist students in becoming AI literate by modeling the responsible use of AI programs that improve student learning outcomes.

- Teachers will be able to save time with the help of AI by automating paperwork and repetitive tasks.

- Teachers can guide students toward understanding AI as a useful tool that is far from perfect or omniscient.

Reflection

Use the following questions to further consider this chapter's new tool and how you can use it to help struggling readers.

1. How might you ensure equitable access to AI tools for all students, especially those with dyslexia or other special needs?

2. What concerns do you have about the growing prominence of AI?

3. What are the potential biases embedded in AI algorithms, and how can we mitigate them in our teaching practice?

4. Have you tried using AI, either personally or in your classroom? If so, what were those experiences like? If not, what apprehensions might you have?

5. Do you think it's possible to responsibly use AI in the classroom without opening ourselves to dangers such as having our voice and image co-opted for other, less desirable purposes?

Reproducible Forms With Suggested Standards and IEP and 504 Goals

The reproducible "Accommodations for Students With Dyslexia That AI Can Help Meet" (page 166) lists accommodations that may be helpful for or even required by an IEP for students with diagnosed dyslexia. Each of these accommodations can be met more easily and quickly by using an AI tool.

Accommodations for Students With Dyslexia That AI Can Help Meet

Accommodations are adjustments that allow a student to demonstrate knowledge, skills, and abilities without lowering learning or performance expectations and without changing what is being measured. *Modifications* change the nature of instruction and assessments and what students are expected to learn. High school teachers need to provide accommodations and modifications for identified learning differences such as dyslexia. With the help of AI, these time-consuming adaptations can be available for all students at all times, relieving the teacher of this task.

Writing the IEP or 504 is the first step in setting accommodations. MagicSchool AI (www.magicschool.ai) offers an IEP generator that allows teachers to fill in information about the student and have a draft IEP with appropriate language generated.

The following list, from the International Dyslexia Association (2020), includes common accommodations or modifications used in IEPs for dyslexia. All of these can be met by allowing students to access various forms of AI. If your school does not already provide the needed AI program, having the program listed as part of the IEP requires the school to provide it.

All the following common accommodations can be met by an AI program or device.

- Verbal instructions
- Repetition of instructions
- Text, including instructions, in audio format
- Larger print
- Dyslexic-friendly font
- Fewer items per page
- Highlighted text
- Information such as facts or definitions in songs or poems
- Extended time
- Timers to keep track of time
- Planners for tracking assignments
- Color coding (for example, subject areas, categorization within notes)
- Putting new learning into own words as soon as possible after class—talking about learning

page 1 of 2

Never Too Late © 2025 Solution Tree Press • SolutionTree.com
Visit **go.SolutionTree.com/literacy** to download this free reproducible.

- Calculator
- Speech-to-text software
- Text-to-speech software
- Electronic dictionary
- Spelling checker
- Grammar checker
- Individual or small group work
- Distraction-free setting
- Flexible scheduling (for example, several sessions rather than one)
- Marking answers on test instead of on separate answer sheet
- Dictating to scribe or record oral responses on audio recorder
- Typing responses
- Reducing visual and auditory distractions
- Allowing for more frequent breaks (as appropriate)
- Changing order of tasks or subtests

References

International Dyslexia Association. (2020). *Accommodations for students with dyslexia.* Accessed at https://dyslexiaida.org/accommodations-for-students-with-dyslexia on June 7, 2024.

EPILOGUE

Early in our careers, as young teachers in an alternative high school, we felt like we were giving up on students who still couldn't read. The problem seemed overwhelming. At the same time, we desperately wanted to help.

We worked with students whose self-esteem and hope were battered. These students had been called "lazy" and "stupid," and now they believed it. They lived in survival mode, lashing out at a world that seemed vastly unfair. Several of our students dropped out of high school because they were sent to jail. This is not unusual. For example, researchers Laura Cassidy, Kayla Reggio, Bennett A. Shaywitz, John M. Holahan, and Sally E. Shaywitz (2021) report that a sample of the U.S. prison population indicates that 47 percent are dyslexic. We came to believe that the hopelessness and frustration experienced by students with dyslexia was at least partially responsible for this sobering statistic.

Eddie, the mechanic with dyslexia we quoted earlier, recalled his high school experience:

> In math, I could often do the problems correctly in my head, but I missed them on the paper because I wrote the answer down backward. I remember a biology class in which I asked the guy in front of me if I could copy his notes after class each day because I just couldn't listen and take notes at the same time. He let me use his notes, and I went from an F to an A by studying my tail off until midnight every night. I was blamed for cheating. (Eddie, personal communication, March 16, 2020)

Neither of us are technical experts. Nor do we have dyslexia. But our students, children, and siblings with dyslexia have taught us that a little bit of technical assistance goes a long way in leveling the field for students with dyslexia. Tech tools play well with dyslexic strengths, allowing these students to flourish academically. As we experimented, we found that the same tools often proved valuable for all students to varying degrees. We learned that making our classrooms friendly to those with dyslexia was good for everyone.

High school teachers expect their students to be able to read. When a student can't read, both the teacher and the student face frustration, and it's easy for one or both of them to give up. You don't need to teach reading to students with dyslexia to help them. You can give students the tools they need to benefit from instruction while, at the same time, improving their reading skills on their own time.

Secondary teachers are expected to meet national, state, and district content standards, curriculum deadlines, and testing requirements while maintaining classroom discipline with large classes. Additionally, increasing numbers of students arrive in class with an IEP or 504 requiring accommodations or modifications. Even if the teacher manages to deliver on those requirements, there are probably students with undiagnosed dyslexia whose needs are not met. This is no time to tell high school teachers to try harder. It's time to give teachers access to tech tools that meet the needs of their highly diverse students. We hope the tech tools in this book will allow you, as a high school teacher in any subject, to dramatically improve outcomes for students with dyslexia without adding to your own workload.

Is high school too late to help students with dyslexia? It's never too late. We've used the research-based techniques in this book to radically change outcomes for teens and adults. We've adapted them over our years of teaching, incorporating new technologies as they emerged. Tech tools can now provide outstanding support for students with dyslexia. Using technology available on smartphones or computers alongside a subtle but powerful shift in handling assignments changes a high school classroom from toxic to triumphant for students who struggle to read.

APPENDIX

In the past, teachers could write short lesson plans and then improvise as needed. Now, thanks to numerous consultants and educational philosophies, teachers may be asked to address a number of specific learning strategies along with standards, IEP goals, and 504 goals in each lesson plan. This is good practice and ups our game as teachers, but can take a lot of time. The following tool is a lesson plan template that can be modified as needed, and can help you save time in addressing a number of learning strategies. You can also go to **go.SolutionTree. com/literacy** to download the reproducible version of the template.

Lesson Plan Template

Unit or topic: _____

Days: _____

Content Standards
List the standards applicable to this unit or topic:

Content Objectives: What are students learning?	**Language Objectives:** How will students learn it?
Essential Questions:	**Bloom's Taxonomy:** Check those that apply. The essential question is . . . ___ Low (Knowledge and Comprehension) ___ Middle (Application and Analysis) ___ High (Synthesis and Evaluation) ___ Psychomotor (Physical Speed and Accuracy)

Building Background

Prior Knowledge: What do students need to know before the lesson?

Key Vocabulary: What are the key terms students need to know to understand the lesson concepts?

Lesson Delivery

Instructional Time:

Lesson Sequence:

Closure:

Materials and Supplies:

WICOR (Writing, Inquiry, Collaboration, Organization, and Reading) Strategies

Depending on the school district, the following instructional strategy responses may be required for a lesson plan. This section includes definitions and sample activities that a district may not provide but could be useful.

Check all that apply and then underline an activity in that category (or give a brief description).

— **Writing** (prewrite, draft, respond, revise, edit, final draft, class and textbook notes, learning logs and journals)

— **Inquiry** (Costa's levels of questions, skilled questioning, Socratic seminars, quick writes and discussion, critical thinking activities, writing questions, open-mindedness activities)

— **Collaboration** (group projects, study groups, jigsaw activities, response-edit-revision activities, collaborative activities)

— **Organization** (tools such as binders, calendars, planners, agendas, graphic organizers, and methods such as focused note-taking system, tutorials, study groups, project planning)

— **Reading** (SQ3R method [survey, question, read, recite, review], KWL charts [what I know, what I want to learn, what I learned], reciprocal teaching, think-alouds, reader response, graphic organizers, vocabulary building)

Strategies		
Check any or all that apply.		
Scaffolding: — Modeling — Guided Practice — Independent Practice	**Describe here if needed:**	**Concept Development:** — Similarities and Differences — Summarizing and Note-Taking — Reinforcing Effort and Providing Recognition — Nonlinguistic Representation — Generating and Testing Hypotheses
Practice and Application: — Listening — Reading — Worksheet — Writing — Discussion — Hands-On or Manipulatives		
Interaction: — Whole Class — Small Group — Partners — Independent	**5E Lesson Planning:** — Engage (capture interest) — Explore (experiment, simulate, or collaborate) — Explain (discuss and define concepts) — Elaborate (apply new knowledge) — Evaluate (assess to gauge comprehension)	**Engaging Qualities:** — Personal Response — Clear and Modeled Expectations — Emotional and Intellectual Safety — Learning With Others — Sense of Audience — Choice — Novelty and Variety — Authenticity

Special Education Requirements

Accommodations—How to Instruct
(to make education more accessible for students with disabilities)

Examples: Timing and scheduling for classwork and tests; reduced-distraction setting; special equipment; presentation in large print; recorded or human-read books; responses using a scribe, graphic organizer, calculator, or speech-to-text equipment

Modifications—What to Instruct
(only for students with an IEP)

Examples: Use fewer concepts, ask different test questions, reduce number of problems, revise assignments, give hints or clues, modify tests, grade on effort, use alternative text and assignments, modify questions, shorten assignments, give open-book tests

Consider each of the following instructional areas. Where appropriate, describe the activity and check whether it was an accommodation or modification.

Instructional Area	Activity	Accommodation	Modification
Content			
Materials			
Delivery			
Activity			

Review and Assessment

Consider the following questions before choosing the assessment:
- How will students receive feedback?
- How do students know what is expected of them?

Check all that apply and provide a brief description.

___ **Formative assessment** (*for* learning; informal)

Examples: Identifying where students are and what their needs are, applying questioning strategies, using exit tickets, checking in with students

___ **Summative assessment** (*of* learning; formal)

Examples: Grading, tests, quizzes, performance tasks, rubrics

Reflection

What do you need to change to facilitate improvement?

What will you do differently if students have not demonstrated mastery of the objective?

What would you add?

Source: AVID. (n.d.). WICOR (writing, inquiry, collaboration, organization, and reading). *Accessed at https:// avidopenaccess.org/wp-content/uploads/2021/08/AVID-WICOR-flyer-080521_proofed.pdf on July 24, 2024;* Echevarría, J., Vogt, M., Short, D. J., & Toppel, K. (2024). Making content comprehensible for multilingual learners: The SIOP model (6th ed.). *Pearson;* Gerges, E. (2022, March 4). How to use the 5E model in your science classroom. *Edutopia. Accessed at www.edutopia.org/article/how-use-5e-model-your-science-classroom on April 9, 2024;* Idaho Special Education Support & Technical Assistance (SESTA). (2022). Idaho IEP guidance handbook: High-quality practices. *Accessed at https://idahotc.com/Portals/0/Resources/1007/The-Idaho-IEP -Guidance-Handbook.pdf on April 9, 2024;* National Governors Association Center for Best Practices & Council of Chief State School Officers. (2010). Common Core State Standards for English language arts and literacy in history/social studies, science, and technical subjects. *Authors. Accessed at https://corestandards.org/wp-content /uploads/2023/09/ELA_Standards1.pdf on January 5, 2025.*

REFERENCES AND RESOURCES

Amazon Web Services. (n.d.). *What is GPT?* Accessed at https://aws.amazon.com/what-is/gpt on July 24, 2024.

AVID. (n.d.). *WICOR (writing, inquiry, collaboration, organization, and reading)*. Accessed at https://avidopenaccess.org/wp-content/uploads/2021/08/AVID-WICOR-flyer-080521_proofed.pdf on July 24, 2024.

Baddeley, S. (2019, December 18). *How I use Voice Typing in my classroom* [Blog post]. Accessed at https://simonbaddeley64.wordpress.com/2019/12/18/how-i-use-voice-typing-in-my-classroom on March 14, 2024.

Barack, L. (2024, March 6). *AI could prove helpful for students with dyslexia*. K–12 Dive. Accessed at www.k12dive.com/news/artificial-intelligence-students-with-dyslexia/709389 on June 5, 2024.

Baruch College. (n.d.). *Speaking rate*. Accessed at https://tfcs.baruch.cuny.edu/speaking%20rate on October 22, 2024.

Bhola, N. (2022). Effect of text-to-speech software on academic achievement of students with dyslexia. *Integrated Journal for Research in Arts and Humanities, 2*(4), 51–55. https://doi.org/10.55544/ijrah.2.4.45

Bonifacci, P., Colombini, E., Marzocchi, M., Tobia, V., & Desideri, L. (2022). Text-to-speech applications to reduce mind wandering in students with dyslexia. *Journal of Computer Assisted Learning, 38*(2), 440–454. https://doi.org/10.1111/jcal.12624

Boninger, F., Molnar, A., & Saldaña, C. (2020, June). *Big claims, little evidence, lots of money: The reality behind the Summit Learning Program and the push to adopt digital personalized learning platforms* [Research brief]. Boulder, CO: National Education Policy Center. Accessed at https://nepc.colorado.edu/sites/default/files/publications/RB%20Summit.pdf on July 24, 2024.

British Dyslexia Association. (n.d.). *Creating a dyslexia friendly workplace.* Accessed at www.bdadyslexia.org.uk/advice/employers/creating-a-dyslexia-friendly-workplace/dyslexia-friendly-style-guide on May 1, 2024.

Cassidy, L., Reggio, K., Shaywitz, B. A., Holahan, J. M., & Shaywitz, S. E. (2021). Dyslexia in incarcerated men and women: A new perspective on reading disability in the prison population. *Journal of Correctional Education, 72*(2), 61–81.

Center for Hearing and Communication. (n.d.). *Recreational noise facts: Playing it loud isn't playing it smart.* Accessed at https://noiseawareness.org/info-center/recreational-noise-facts on April 26, 2024.

Chong-White, N., Mejia, J., & Edwards, B. (2023, June 12). *Evaluating Apple Air Pods Pro 2 hearing protection and listening* [Blog post]. The Hearing Review. Accessed at https://hearingreview.com/inside-hearing/research/evaluating-apple-airpods-pro-2-for-hearing-protection-and-listening on October 22, 2024.

Clinton-Lisell, V. (2023). Does reading while listening to text improve comprehension compared to reading only? A systematic review and meta-analysis. *Educational Research: Theory and Practice, 34*(3), 133–155.

Cubillas, T. E., & Cangke, M. S. (2023). Amplification of reading fluency among grade 8 students in English through audio-assisted reading strategy. *International Journal of Membrane Science and Technology, 10*(2), 728–737.

Dalhousie University Libraries. (n.d.). *Citation style guide: Citing artificial intelligence.* Accessed at https://dal.ca.libguides.com/CitationStyleGuide/citing-ai on June 6, 2024.

Daniel, B. K., & Bird, R. (2019). Attention! Student voice: Providing students with digital learning materials before scheduled lectures improves learning experience. *Turkish Online Journal of Educational Technology, 18*(3), 1–9.

Davenport University Library. (2023). *Learning domains.* Accessed at https://davenport.libguides.com/learningoutcomes/domains on April 9, 2024.

Dixon-Román, E., Nichols, T. P., & Nyame-Mensah, A. (2020). The racializing forces of/in AI educational technologies. *Learning, Media and Technology, 45*(3), 236–250. https://doi.org/10.1080/17439884.2020.1667825

DuFour, R., DuFour, R., Eaker, R., Many, T., Mattos, M., & Muhammad, A. (2024). *Learning by doing: A handbook for Professional Learning Communities at Work* (4th ed.). Solution Tree Press.

DyslexiaHelp. (n.d.a). *Dr. Maggie Aderin-Pocock.* Accessed at https://dyslexiahelp.umich.edu/success-stories/dr-maggie-aderin-pocock on April 9, 2024.

DyslexiaHelp. (n.d.b). *10 helpful text-to-speech readers for back to school.* Accessed at https://dyslexiahelp.umich.edu/tools/software-assistive-technology/text-to-speech-readers on March 8, 2024.

Dyslexic Advantage. (2021). *Mind wandering, reading, and dyslexia.* Accessed at www.dyslexicadvantage.org/mind-wandering-reading-and-dyslexia on March 6, 2024.

Dyslexic Advantage. (2023, May 16). *What about audiobooks? Chat with dyslexia kit author and educator Yvonna Graham* [Video file]. Accessed at www.youtube.com/watch?v=aAyb4LRH3Eo on March 1, 2024.

Echevarría, J., Vogt, M., Short, D. J., & Toppel, K. (2024). *Making content comprehensible for multilingual learners: The SIOP model* (6th ed.). Pearson.

Education Week. (2023, January 30). *What is background knowledge, and how does it fit into the science of reading?* Accessed at www.edweek.org/teaching-learning/what-is-background-knowledge-and-how-does-it-fit-into-the-science-of-reading/2023/01 on March 24, 2024.

Eide, B. L., & Eide, F. F. (2020, May 26). *Stealth dyslexia: Gifted parenting and strategies* [Blog post]. Davidson Institute. Accessed at www.davidsongifted.org/gifted-blog/stealth-dyslexia on April 1, 2024.

Eide, B. L., & Eide, F. F. (2023). *The dyslexic advantage: Unlocking the hidden potential of the dyslexic brain* (Rev. ed.). Plume.

Elamadurthi, R. K., Pavani G., KanthiThilaka, J. M., Pavani, A., Ravichand, M., & Seshagiri, H. (2023). Improve students reading skills via the use of computer-assisted reading programmes. In *2023 International Conference on Advances in Computing, Communication and Applied Informatics (ACCAI)* (pp. 1–6). Institute of Electrical and Electronics Engineers. https://doi.org/10.1109/ACCAI58221.2023.10201220

Family Educational Rights and Privacy Act, 20 U.S.C. § 1232g, 34 CFR Part 99 (1988).

Fischer, C., Pardos, Z. A., Baker, R. S., Williams, J. J., Smyth, P., Yu, R., et al. (2020). Mining big data in education: Affordances and challenges. *Review of Research in Education, 44*(1), 130–160. https://doi.org/10.3102/0091732X20903304

Fishel, T., & Fishel, J. (2021). *How Tony learned to read: Growing up dyslexic.* Flying Heron Books.

Frankenberger, C. (n.d.). *Livescribe smartpen.* Accessed at https://dyslexia.yale.edu/resources/tools-technology/tech-tips/livescribe-smartpen on May 18, 2024.

Foxwell, A. (2023, July 27). *5 assistive technology tools for students with dyslexia* [Blog post]. Accessed at www.readspeaker.com/blog/assistive-technology-for-dyslexia on March 23, 20204.

Gath, M. E., Monk, L., Scott, A., & Gillon, G. T. (2024). Smartphones at school: A mixed-methods analysis of educators' and students' perspectives on mobile phone use at school. *Education Sciences, 14*(4), 351. https://doi.org/10.3390/educsci14040351

Gerges, E. (2022, March 4). *How to use the 5E model in your science classroom.* Edutopia. Accessed at www.edutopia.org/article/how-use-5e-model-your-science-classroom on April 9, 2024.

Glassman, S. (2021, October 16). The best assistive technology for dyslexics. *Wired.* Accessed at www.wired.com/story/the-best-assistive-technology-dyslexia on March 8, 2024.

Goel, A., Joyner, D., & Rugaber, S. (n.d.). *Virtual teaching assistant: Jill Watson.* Georgia Tech GVU Center. Accessed at https://gvu.gatech.edu/research/projects/virtual-teaching-assistant-jill-watson on October 22, 2024.

Goldstone, L., Lazarus, S. S., Olson, R., Hinkle, A. R., & Ressa, V. A. (2021). *Speech-to-text: Research (NCEO accommodations toolkit 16*a). National Center on Educational Outcomes. Accessed at https://publications.ici.umn.edu/nceo/accommodations-toolkit/speech-to-text-research on July 25, 2024.

Goodacre, C. (2018, November 1). *Why I still flip* [Blog post]. Accessed at https://flippedmathclass.blogspot.com/2018/11/why-i-still-flip.html on October 22, 2024.

Gorelik, K. (2017, October 26). *7 ways audiobooks benefit students who struggle with reading* [Blog post]. Accessed at www.weareteachers.com/audiobooks-benefit-students on April 17, 2024.

Graham, Y. (2022, February 27). *Teaching yourself to read part 1: Fishel & Graham interview* [Video file]. Accessed at www.youtube.com/watch?v=EDFYxfsUijo&t=245s on July 25, 2024.

Graham, Y., & Graham, A. E. (2021). *Dyslexia tool kit: What to do when phonics isn't enough* (Expanded ed.). Self-published.

Greenwald, W. (2024, June 27). The best smart glasses for 2024. *PCMag.* Accessed at www.pcmag.com/picks/the-best-smart-glasses on June 3, 2024.

Griggs, K. (2022). *This is dyslexia: The definitive guide to the untapped power of dyslexic thinking and its vital role in our future.* Vermilion.

Grusky, M., Taft, J. G., Naaman, M., & Azenkot, S. (2020). Measuring and understanding online reading behaviors of people with dyslexia. In R. Bernhaupt, F. Mueller, D. Verweij, J. Andres, J. McGrenere, A. Cockburn, et al. (Eds.), *CHI '20: Proceedings of the 2020 CHI Conference on Human Factors in Computing Systems.* Association for Computing Machinery. https://doi.org/10.1145/3313831

Hearing Health Foundation. (n.d.). *Headphone and earbud safety.* Accessed at https://hearinghealthfoundation.org/keeplistening/headphones on May 5, 2024.

Heaven, W. D. (2023, November 16). Google DeepMind wants to define what counts as artificial general intelligence. *MIT Technology Review.* Accessed at www.technologyreview.com/2023/11/16/1083498/google-deepmind-what-is-artificial-general-intelligence-agi on May 31, 2024.

Higham, A. (2024, September 23). Do not disturb: Mobile phone ban sweeps American schools. *Newsweek.* Accessed at www.newsweek.com/do-not-disturb-mobile-phone-ban-american-schools-1953348#:~:text=Across%20the%20country%2C%20some%2076,the%20school%20or%20its%20district. on October 21, 2024.

House of Marley. (2023, July 13). *12 different types of headphones explained* [Blog post]. Accessed at www.thehouseofmarley.com/blog/types-of-headphones on April 2, 2024.

Hughes, A. (2023, June 14). Jobs need skills, not degrees. *Forbes.* Accessed at www.forbes.com/sites/forbestechcouncil/2023/06/14/jobs-need-skills-not-degrees/?sh=7a36da941bb6 on June 6, 2024.

IBM. (2023). *What are AI hallucinations?* Accessed at www.ibm.com/topics/ai-hallucinations on June 3, 2024.

Idaho Special Education Support & Technical Assistance (SESTA). (2022). *Idaho IEP guidance handbook: High-quality practices.* Accessed at https://idahotc.com/Portals/0/Resources/1007/The-Idaho-IEP-Guidance-Handbook.pdf on April 9, 2024.

International Dyslexia Association. (2020a). *Accommodations for students with dyslexia.* Accessed at https://dyslexiaida.org/accommodations-for-students-with-dyslexia on June 7, 2024.

International Dyslexia Association. (2020b). *Understanding dysgraphia.* Accessed at https://dyslexiaida.org/understanding-dysgraphia on March 14, 2024.

Katz, L. (2024). *Bone conduction headphones: Gimmick or godsend?* Accessed at soundguys.com/bone-conduction-headphones-20580 on October 19, 2024.

Keelor, J. L., Creaghead, N., Silbert, N., & Horowitz-Kraus, T. (2020). Text-to-speech technology: Enhancing reading comprehension for students with reading difficulty. *Assistive technology outcomes and benefits, 14,* 19–35.

Khan, S. (2024). *Brave new words: How AI will revolutionize education (and why that's a good thing).* Viking.

Khanmigo. (n.d.). *Meet Khanmigo: Your free, AI-powered teaching assistant.* Accessed at www.khanmigo.ai/teachers on June 3, 2024.

Kim, J. (2024, September 14). *FDA approves some Apple AirPods to be used as hearing aids*. National Public Radio. Accessed at www.npr.org/2024/09/14/nx-s1-5112400/fda-airpods-hearing-aids-software-update on October 23, 2024.

Knoop-van Campen, C. A. N. (2022). *Multimedia learning and dyslexia* [Doctoral dissertation, Radboud University]. Behavioral Science Institute. Accessed at https://carolienknoopvancampen.nl/onewebmedia/Proefschrift%20Carolien%20Knoop-van%20Campen.pdf on April 15, 2024.

Knoop-van Campen, C. A. N., ter Doest, D., Verhoeven, L., & Segers, E. (2022). The effect of audio-support on strategy, time, and performance on reading comprehension in secondary school students with dyslexia. *Annals of Dyslexia, 72*(2), 341–360.

Knox, J. (2020). Artificial intelligence and education in China. *Learning, Media and Technology, 45*(3), 298–311. https://doi.org/10.1080/17439884.2020.1754236

Knox, J., Williamson, B., & Bayne, S. (2020). Machine behaviourism: Future visions of 'learnification' and 'datafication' across humans and digital technologies. *Learning, Media and Technology, 45*(1), 31–45.

Koenig, R. (2021, October 27). *The pandemic pushed colleges to record lectures. The practice may be here to stay*. EdSurge. Accessed at www.edsurge.com/news/2021-10-27-the-pandemic-pushed-colleges-to-record-lectures-the-practice-may-be-here-to-stay on June 24, 2024.

Kulawiak, P. R. (2021). Academic benefits of wearing noise-cancelling headphones during class for typically developing students and students with special needs: A scoping review. *Cogent Education, 8*(1), Article 1957530. https://doi.org/10.1080/2331186X.2021.1957530

Landmark School. (2023, June 5). *EdChat, Josh Clark interview Chris Dede* [Video file]. Accessed at www.youtube.com/watch?v=gsnz1uGoTTg on June 24, 2024.

Langreo, L. (2024, January 5). *Teachers told us they've used AI in the classroom. Here's why*. Education Week. Accessed at www.edweek.org/technology/teachers-told-us-theyve-used-ai-in-the-classroom-heres-why/2024/01 on April 3, 2024.

Levine, S., Hsieh, H., Southerton, E., & Silverman, R. (2023). How high school students used speech-to-text as a composition tool. *Computers and Composition, 68*, Article 102775. https://doi.org/10.1016/j.compcom.2023.102775

Lovett, B. J. (2021). Educational accommodations for students with disabilities: Two equity-related concerns. *Frontiers in Education, 6*. https://doi.org/10.3389/feduc.2021.795266

Made by Dyslexia. (n.d.). *5 ways technology helps dyslexics in the workplace*. Accessed at www.madebydyslexia.org/wp-content/uploads/5-ways-technology-helps-dyslexics.pdf on March 2, 2024.

Made by Dyslexia. (2022). *Dyslexia: The school report*. Accessed at www.madebydyslexia.org/wp-content/uploads/Dyslexia-The-School-Report.pdf on March 18, 2024.

Made by Dyslexia. (2024). *Intelligence 5.0: A new school of thought rethinking the intelligence needed in industry 5.0*. Accessed at www.madebydyslexia.org/MBD-Intelligence-5.0-Report.pdf on October 21, 2024.

Martha Bradley Evans Center for Teaching Excellence. (n.d.). *Bloom's taxonomy: Revised for 21st-century learners*. Accessed at https://cte.utah.edu/instructor-education/Blooms-Taxonomy.php on April 9, 2024.

Martineau, K. (2023, April 20). *What is generative AI?* [Blog post]. Accessed at https://research.ibm.com/blog/what-is-generative-AI on October 21, 2024.

Matre, M. E., & Cameron, D. L. (2024). A scoping review on the use of speech-to-text technology for adolescents with learning difficulties in secondary education. *Disability and Rehabilitation: Assistive Technology, 19*(3), 1103–1116.

McStay, A. (2020). Emotional AI and EdTech: Serving the public good? *Learning, Media and Technology, 45*(3), 270–283. https://doi.org/10.1080/17439884.2020.1686016

Merritt, R. (2022, March 25). *What is a transformer model?* [Blog post]. Accessed at https://blogs.nvidia.com/blog/what-is-a-transformer-model on June 3, 2024.

MIT Management. (n.d.). *When AI gets it wrong: Addressing AI hallucinations and bias*. Accessed at https://mitsloanedtech.mit.edu/ai/basics/addressing-ai-hallucinations-and-bias on September 19, 2024.

Montgomery, J. W., Gillam, R. B., & Evans, J. L. (2021). A new memory perspective on the sentence comprehension deficits of school-age children with developmental language disorder: Implications for theory, assessment, and intervention. *Language, Speech, and Hearing Services in Schools, 52*(2), 449–466.

Mucci, T., & Stryker, C. (2024). *Getting ready for artificial general intelligence with example*. Accessed at www.ibm.com/think/topics/artificial-general-intelligence-examples on October 21, 2024.

National Governors Association Center for Best Practices & Council of Chief State School Officers. (2010). *Common Core State Standards for English language arts and literacy in history/social studies, science, and technical subjects*. Authors. Accessed at https://corestandards.org/wp-content/uploads/2023/09/ELA_Standards1.pdf on January 5, 2025.

National University. (n.d.). *Can music help you study and focus?* [Blog post]. Accessed at www.nu.edu/blog/can-music-help-you-study-and-focus on May 5, 2024.

Nightingale, K. P., Anderson, V., Onens, S., Fazil, Q., & Davies, H. (2019). Developing the inclusive curriculum: Is supplementary lecture recording an effective approach in supporting students with Specific Learning Difficulties (SpLDs)? *Computers & Education, 130*, 13–25. https://doi.org/10.1016/j.compedu.2018.11.006

Nkomo, L. M., & Daniel, B. K. (2021). Providing students with flexible and adaptive learning opportunities using lecture recordings. *Journal of Open, Flexible and Distance Learning, 25*(1), 22–31. doi:10.61468/jofdl.v25i1.437

North Carolina University at Charlotte Office of Legal Affairs. (n.d.). *Classroom recordings and FERPA: FAQs*. Accessed at https://legal.charlotte.edu/legal-topics/classroom-policies-and-practices/classroom-recordings-and-ferpa-faqs on May 18, 2024.

Northwood Tech Innovative Teaching and Learning Center. (n.d.). *Artificial intelligence introduction*. Accessed at https://itlc.northwoodtech.edu/introduction/ai/llm on October 21, 2024.

Occupational Safety and Health Administration. (n.d.). *Occupational noise exposure*. Accessed at www.osha.gov/noise on July 25, 2024.

OpenDyslexic. (n.d.). *About*. Accessed at https://opendyslexic.org/about on December 12, 2024.

Owens, D. (n.d.). *What is ITS?* Accessed at https://infosystems.utdallas.edu/voices/information-systems-articles/information-technology-and-systems-articles/what-is-its on June 2, 2024.

Plosz, J. (n.d.). *Discussion of Casanova's comparison related to teaching*. Accessed at www.academia.edu/31973901/Discussion_of_Casanovas_comparison_related_to_teaching_pdf on March 1, 2024.

Ramsey, K. (2020, October 28). *The benefits of video for students with dyslexia* [Blog post]. Accessed at www.boclips.com/blog/the-benefits-of-video-for-students-with-dyslexia on October 20, 2024.

Reading Rockets. (n.d.a). *Audio-assisted reading.* Accessed at www.readingrockets.org/classroom/classroom-strategies/audio-assisted-reading on October 17, 2024.

Reading Rockets. (n.d.b). *Text-to-speech technology: What it is and how it works.* Accessed at www.readingrockets.org/topics/assistive-technology/articles/text-speech-technology-what-it-and-how-it-works on October 18, 2024.

Redford, K. (n.d.). *How teachers can build a word-rich life for dyslexics.* Accessed at https://dyslexia.yale.edu/resources/educators/school-culture/building-a-word-rich-life-for-dyslexics on October 16, 2024.

Reitman, H. (Host). (2016, May 10). The dyslexic astrophysicist, Dr. Matthew Schneps [Audio podcast episode]. In *Exploring different brains.* Accessed at https://differentbrains.org/the-dyslexic-astrophysicist-dr-matthew-schneps-exploring-different-brains-episode-22 on July 25, 2024.

Robinson, K., & Aronica, L. (2015). *Creative schools: The grassroots revolution that's transforming education.* Viking.

Ross, H. M. (n.d.). AI in the classroom—Helping or hurting? *Washington FAMILY.* Accessed at www.washingtonfamily.com/ai-in-classrooms on June 5, 2024.

Russell, M. (2024, April 28). *What I learned by recording my classes* [Blog post]. Accessed at www.middleweb.com/34434/recording-your-class-may-prompt-powerful-reflection/?unapproved=453334&moderation-hash=6d8c472fdbb309de338fe1782cbd87a5#comment-453334 on October 20, 2024.

Salza, L., & Alexander, J. (2019). Great debate: What is the role of AT for students with dyslexia? *Examiner, 8*(1). Accessed at https://dyslexiaida.org/great-debate-what-is-the-role-of-at-for-students-with-dyslexia/#:~:text=In%20short%2C%20assistive%20technology%20can,his%20or%20her%20well%2Dbeing. on December 11, 2024.

Schultz, S. (2022). *Differences between a 504 plan and an Individualized Education Program (IEP)* Accessed at www.nea.org/professional-excellence/student-engagement/tools-tips/differences-between-504-plan-and-individualized-education-program-iep on October 23, 2024.

Shaywitz, S. (2020). *Overcoming dyslexia* (2nd ed.). Knopf.

Smith, S. (2021, March 23). *School headphones in class can be brilliant: Here's why* [Blog post]. Accessed at https://learningheadphones.com/blogs/school-headphone-blog/school-headphones-in-class-can-be-brilliant-here-s-why on April 19, 2024.

Soft dB. (2019, May 14). *Measurement in decibels: What is the difference between dB and dB(A)?* [Blog post]. Accessed at www.softdb.com/blog/difference-between-db-dba on October 23, 2024.

Stanford Medicine. (2007, August 1). *Music moves brain to pay attention, Stanford study finds.* Accessed at https://med.stanford.edu/news/all-news/2007/07/music-moves-brain-to-pay-attention-stanford-study-finds.html on December 4, 2024.

Stanford Alumni. (2021, November 19). *Emerging brain computer interfaces with Krishna Shenoy* [Video file]. Accessed at www.youtube.com/watch?v=XRw3Jt4Qr2Y on June 3, 2024.

Stark, K. (2016). *When strangers meet: How people you don't know can transform you.* TED Books.

Stim, R. (n.d.). *Grading teachers on copyright law—Video recording for the classroom.* Accessed at https://fairuse.stanford.edu/overview/faqs/videotaping on May 18, 2024.

Strait, E. (2023, March 31). *Understanding NLP history: The evolution of speech recognition* [Blog post]. Accessed at www.lettria.com/blogpost/understanding-nlp-history-the-evolution-of-speech-recognition on July 25, 2024.

Taylor, D., Yeung, M., & Bashet, A. Z. (2021). Personalized and adaptive learning. In J. Ryoo & K. Winkelmann (Eds.), *Innovative learning environments in STEM higher education: Opportunities, challenges, and looking forward* (pp. 17–34). Springer. Accessed at https://library.oapen.org/bitstream/handle/20.500.12657/47325/1/9783030589486.pdf#page=31 on October 22, 2024.

Terada, Y. (2022, November 11). *Six research-backed reasons to record important lessons*. Edutopia. Accessed at www.edutopia.org/article/why-you-should-be-recording-your-lectures on October 21, 2024.

Topale, L. (2016). The strategic use of lecture recordings to facilitate an active and self-directed learning approach. *BMC Medical Education*, *16*(1), Article 201. https://doi.org/10.1186/s12909-016-0723-0

Townsley, M., & Wear, N. L. (2020). *Making grades matter: Standards-based grading in a secondary PLC at Work*. Solution Tree Press.

Undivided. (2024, April 3). *List of accommodations for IEPs and 504s*. Accessed at https://undivided.io/resources/list-of-accommodations-for-ieps-and-504s-210 on May 20, 2024.

Université de Genève. (2022, January 17). *Improving reading skills through action video games*. ScienceDaily. Accessed at www.sciencedaily.com/releases/2022/01/220117115113.htm on April 17, 2024.

Van Hirtum, T., Ghesquière, P., & Wouters, J. (2021). A bridge over troubled listening: Improving speech-in-noise perception by children with dyslexia. *Journal of the Association for Research in Otolaryngology*, *22*(4), 465–480. https://doi.org/10.1007/s10162-021-00793-4

Venger, I. (2024, January 27). *How a bunch of high schoolers surprised me with their take on AI* [Blog post]. Accessed at https://medium.com/@ilya.venger/how-a-bunch-of-high-schoolers-surprised-me-with-their-take-on-ai-caeb13cfb4c1 on July 25, 2024.

Voice Dream. (n.d.). *Reading reinvented*. Accessed at www.voicedream.com/reader on October 23, 2024.

Voice Dream. (2013, May 6). *Universal access for the written word* [Blog post]. Accessed at www.voicedream.com/universal-access-for-the-written-word on April 21, 2024.

Voice Dream. (2014, September 8). *How one dyslexic speed reads* [Blog post]. Accessed at www.voicedream.com/how-one-dyslexic-speed-reads on April 16, 2024.

Wafer, L. (n.d.). *Five ways lesson recording transformed my teaching practice* [Blog post]. Accessed at www.hovercam.com/blog/5-ways-lesson-recording-transformed-my-teaching-practice on May 21, 2024.

Wang, J., Dawson, K., Saunders, K., Ritzhaupt, A. D., Antonenko, P., Lombardino, L., et al. (2018). Investigating the effects of modality and multimedia on the learning performance of college students with dyslexia. *Journal of Special Education Technology*, *33*(3), 182–193. https://doi.org/10.1177/0162643418754530

Wang, L. M., & Brill, L. C. (2021). Speech and noise levels measured in occupied K–12 classrooms. *The Journal of the Acoustical Society of America*, *150*(2), 864–877.

Warren, E. (2016, June 3). *Dyslexia and Voice Dream Reader: A demonstration and discussion with Stan Gloss and Dr. Erica Warren* [Video file]. Accessed at www.youtube.com/watch?v=5cdVCQoiTqU on October 16, 2024.

Weitzman, C. (2022a, November 10). *Audio books under 5 hours* [Blog post]. Accessed at https://speechify.com/blog/average-length-of-an-audiobook/ on October 23, 2024.

Weitzman, C. (2022b, June 2). *Text-to-speech for dyslexia: What you need to know* [Blog post]. Accessed at https://speechify.com/blog/text-to-speech-dyslexia on October 23, 2024.

Whitten, C., Labby, S., & Sullivan, S. L. (2016). The impact of pleasure reading on academic success. *The Journal of Multidisciplinary Graduate Research*, *2*(4), 48–64.

Williamson, B., & Eynon, R. (2020). Historical threads, missing links, and future directions in AI in education. *Learning, Media and Technology*, *45*(3), 223–235. https://doi.org/10.1080/17439884.2020.1798995

Wood, S. G., Moxley, J. H., Tighe, E. L., & Wagner, R. K. (2018). Does use of text-to-speech and related read-aloud tools improve reading comprehension for students with reading disabilities? A meta-analysis. *Journal of Learning Disabilities*, *51*(1), 73–84. https://doi.org/10.1177/0022219416688170

Yale Center for Dyslexia & Creativity. (n.d.a). *Maggie Aderin-Pocock, Ph.D., space scientist & science communicator*. Accessed at https://dyslexia.yale.edu/story/maggie-aderin-pocock-ph-d on March 12, 2024.

Yale Center for Dyslexia & Creativity. (n.d.b). *See what learners are saying about overcoming dyslexia on Coursera!* Accessed at www.dyslexia.yale.edu/learner-reviews on December 15, 2024.

Yale Center for Dyslexia & Creativity. (n.d.c). *Tips from students*. Accessed at https://dyslexia.yale.edu/resources/dyslexic-kids-adults/tips-from-students on April 23, 2024.

Yale University. (n.d.). *Student accessibility services*. Accessed at https://sas.yale.edu/assistive-technologies/text-to-speech on March 8, 2024.

Zakiyuddin, Z., Mustofa, M., & Yunus, M. (2022). The effect of using computer-assisted reading with inquiry-based learning on student reading comprehension. *English Education Journal*, *13*(1), 122–139. https://doi.org/10.24815/eej.v13i1.25164

Zingoni, A., Taborri, J., Panetti, V., Bonechi, S., Aparicio-Martínez, P., Pinzi, S., et al. (2021). Investigating issues and needs of dyslexia students at university: Proof of concept of an artificial intelligence and virtual reality-based supporting platform and preliminary results. *Applied Sciences*, *11*(10), Article 4624. https://doi.org/10.3390/app11104624

INDEX

NUMBERS

504 plans

    about, 11

    artificial intelligence and, 164, 165

    headphones and, 121, 122

    recorded lessons and, 141, 142

    reproducibles for, 143–144

    speech-to-text tools and, 61, 62, 63

    text-to-speech tools and, 38–39

    tracking with audio-assisted reading and, 91–92

A

accommodations

    IEP and 504 accommodations, 11

    reproducibles for, 166–167

    text-to-speech tools and, 32, 33

    use of term, 39

    videos as, 128

active noise cancellation (ANC), 105. *See also* headphones, use of

adaptive learning, 151–152. *See also* artificial intelligence (AI)

Aderin-Pocock, M., 23

Adobe Acrobat Reader, 28. *See also* text-to-speech tools

algorithms, 152. *See also* artificial intelligence (AI)

anxiety, 120

Apple AirPods, 113–114. *See also* headphones, use of

Apple Spoken Content, 28. *See also* text-to-speech tools

artificial general intelligence (AGI), 150, 152

artificial intelligence (AI)
    about, 147–149
    and addressing pushback, 162–164
    AI literacy, 159
    citations for, 163–164
    classroom applications of, 157–162
    and helping students with dyslexia, 154–157
    and lesson planning, 160, 161–162
    and recorded lessons, 138
    reproducibles for, 166–167
    summary, 164–165
    vocabulary of, 151–153
    what artificial intelligence is, 149–151

audio support, use of term, 75

audio-assisted reading, use of term, 75

audiobooks
    headphones and, 109
    recording your textbook, 88
    text-to-speech tools and, 25, 34–35, 36
    tracking with audio-assisted reading and, 73–74, 83, 89–90

autism, dyslexia and autism differences in brain structure, 5

B

Baddeley, S., 59

Bashet, A., 151–152

Bhola, N., 27

bone conduction headphones, 105. *See also* headphones, use of

Bonifacci, P., 29

brain development, 3–4, 5

brain-machine interface (BMI), 153. *See also* artificial intelligence (AI)

Brill, L., 108

C

Cameron, D., 54

Casanova, M., 4

cell phones
    artificial intelligence and, 163
    recorded lessons and, 131–132, 137–138

Center for Hearing and Communication, 106

ChatGPT, 152, 153, 157. *See also* artificial intelligence (AI)

Chen, W., 79

Chong-White, N., 113

citations and artificial intelligence, 163–164

classroom management and recorded lessons, 135

closed-back headphones, 105. *See also* headphones, use of

cognitive load
    decoding and, 29, 78
    headphones and, 113
    recorded lessons and, 128
    speech-to-text tools and, 53

comprehension
    headphones and, 116
    speech-to-text tools and, 54
    text-to-speech tools and, 26, 28–29, 30, 32, 37
    tracking with audio-assisted reading and, 77, 78, 79

computers and video recordings, 132–133. *See also* recorded lessons

connections, making connections and dyslexia as a superpower, 4 copyright and recorded lessons, 139

D

Daniel, B., 129

decoding

    cognitive load and, 29, 78

    comprehension and, 30

Descript, 138.
See also recorded lessons

dictation technology, use of term, 51

Dragon Naturally Speaking, 38, 51, 60–61.
See also speech-to-text tools

dysgraphia, 52, 128

dyslexia

    brain structure, difference in dyslexia and autism, 5

    as a hidden superpower, 3–6

    prevalence of, 3, 6–8

Dyslexic Advantage: Unlocking the Hidden Potential of the Dyslexic Brain, The (Eide and Eide), 4

E

earbuds, 105.
See also headphones, use of

editing

    small-group editing, 55–56

    speech-to-text editing checklist, 58

EdPuzzle, 138.
See also recorded lessons

Edwards, B., 113

Eide, B., 4, 49, 52

Eide, F., 4, 49, 52

enhanced envelope (EE) audio, 112.
See also headphones, use of

F

focused reading mode, 76–77

font, OpenDyslexic font, 76

Frankenberger, C., 130

G

Gath, M., 131

generative AI, 149, 150, 152.
See also artificial intelligence (AI)

generative pretrained transformers (GPT), 152.
See also artificial intelligence (AI)

Gillon, G., 131

Goel, A., 152

Goldstone, L., 53

Google, 32, 51, 59, 148.
See also artificial intelligence (AI); speech-to-text tools

Grammarly, 58.
See also artificial intelligence (AI); editing

Griggs, K., 35

H

hallucinations, 150, 152, 154.
See also artificial intelligence (AI)

headphones, use of

    about, 103–104

    and addressing pushback, 119–121

    classroom applications of, 114–119

    and helping students with dyslexia, 106–114

    and reading for pleasure, 110–114

    recommendations for, 118–119

    student to student use of, 110

    summary, 121–122

    types of, 104–106

hearing loss, 84, 107, 113, 120

Higgs, M., 157

Higham, A., 132

Hinkle, A., 53

Hirtum, V., 113

homework
    artificial intelligence and, 160
    recorded lessons and, 135, 140, 141
    text-to-speech tools and, 25

I

IEPs (individualized education plans)
    about, 11
    artificial intelligence and, 164, 165
    headphones and, 121, 122
    recorded lessons and, 141, 142
    reproducibles for, 143–144
    speech-to-text tools and, 61, 62, 63
    text-to-speech tools and, 38–39
    tracking with audio-assisted reading and, 91–92

immersive reading, use of term, 75

implementing recorded lessons. *See* recorded lessons

in-ear monitors (IEMs), 105. *See also* headphones, use of

interventions and text-to-speech tools, 26

in-text citations and artificial intelligence, 163

introduction
    about this book, 11–12
    dyslexia as a hidden superpower, 3–6
    five main ideas, 12–13
    need for classroom tools, 8–11
    prevalence of dyslexia, 6–8
    reproducibles for, 16–20
    what's in this book, 13–15

J

Januski, A., 50

Jill Watson, 152. *See also* artificial intelligence (AI)

Joyner, D., 152

K

Khan, S., 161

Khan Academy and Khanmigo, 151, 158. *See also* artificial intelligence (AI)

Knoop-Van Campen, C., 78, 80

Kulawiak, R., 110

Kurzweil 3000, 27. *See also* text-to-speech tools

L

Labby, S., 111

Langreo, L., 155

large language models (LLMs), 153. *See also* artificial intelligence (AI)

Lazarus, S., 53

Learning Ally, 28, 36. *See also* text-to-speech tools

libraries, building a curricula-aligned digital and physical multimedia library, 85. *See also* audiobooks; recorded lessons

listening, tracking with audio-assisted reading and, 82–83, 89–90

Lovett, B., 33

M

Matre, M., 54

Mejia, J., 113

Merritt, R., 153

Microsoft software, 27–28, 59, 76. *See also* text-to-speech tools; tracking with audio-assisted reading

modifications, use of term, 39

Monk, L., 131

Mucci, T., 150

music
- and addressing pushback, 119–120
- making friends with, 114–116
- for studying, 111–112

N

National University, 111, 112

NaturalReader, 27. *See also* text-to-speech tools

neural interfaces (NIs), 153. *See also* artificial intelligence (AI)

Nkomo, L., 129

noise-canceling headphones, 105. *See also* headphones, use of

O

Occupational Safety and Health Administration, 107, 109

Olson, R., 53

on-ear headphones, 104. *See also* headphones, use of

open-back headphones, 105. *See also* headphones, use of

OpenDyslexic font, 76

over-ear headphones, 104. *See also* headphones, use of

P

patterns, recognizing and dyslexia as a hidden superpower, 4

pens
- scanning pens, 28, 33–34
- smart pens, 130–131

permissions for recording, 136–137

Planck, M., 153

R

Ramsey, K., 128

read-aloud technology, use of term, 24

reading for pleasure, 110–114

reading instruction and dyslexia, 8

reading while listening (RWL), use of term, 75. *See also* tracking with audio-assisted reading

recorded lessons
- about, 125–126
- and addressing pushback, 139–141
- classroom applications of, 133–139
- and helping students with dyslexia, 127–133
- improving teaching experience with, 134–135
- jazzing up productions, 138–139
- permissions for recording, 136–137
- recording devices, types of, 130–133
- reproducibles for, 143–144
- summary, 141–142
- what recorded lessons are, 126–127

Redford, K., 29, 81, 83

reference lists and artificial intelligence, 164

reproducibles for
- accommodations for students with dyslexia that AI can meet, 166–167
- common IEP and 504 goals that lesson recording may meet, 143–144
- lesson plan template, 174–179
- sample speech-to-text lesson plan, 64–70
- sample text-to-speech lesson plan, 40–46

sample tracking lesson plan, 93–100

seeing through the invisibility cloak, 16–20

resources. *See also specific tools*

need for classroom tools, 8–11

prevalence of dyslexia and, 7

Ressa, V., 53

reteaching lessons, 135

Ross, H., 156

Rugaber, S., 152

Russell, M., 125

S

scanning pens, 28, 33–34. *See also* text-to-speech tools

Schwartz, S., 30

Scott, A., 131

self-assessments, 25

self-reflection, 134–135

semi-open headphones, 106. *See also* headphones, use of

signal-to-noise ratio, 108, 109

small-group editing, 57–58

smart pens, 130–131

smartphones, 131–132, 137–138. *See also* cell phones

Smith, S., 107

Soft dB, 106

Speechify, 28, 32. *See also* text-to-speech tools

speech-to-text tool

about, 49–50

and addressing pushback, 59–61

classroom applications of, 55–59

and helping students with dyslexia, 52–54

reproducibles for, 64–70

speech-to-text tools friendly classrooms, 56–57

summary, 61–63

what is speech-to-text, 51–52

spelling

dysgraphia and, 52

Grammarly and, 58

speech-to-text tools and, 49–50, 53, 54, 55–56

Stim, R., 139

subtitles and captions, 84, 87

Sullivan, S., 111

T

Taylor, D., 151–152

tests and testing

artificial intelligence and, 150, 156

vocabulary and, 29

textbooks

recorded lessons and, 139

recording your textbook, 88

text-to-speech tools and, 35–36

tracking with audio-assisted reading and, 89

text-to-speech tools

about, 23–24

access to, 33–34

and addressing pushback, 35–36

classroom applications of, 31–35

and helping students with dyslexia, 25–31

reproducibles for, 40–46

Index | 197

and sharing technical skills, 34

summary, 37–39

what is text-to-speech, 24–25

tracking with audio-assisted reading

about, 73–74

and addressing pushback, 89–90

building a curricula-aligned digital and physical multimedia library, 85

buy-in, seeking, 85–86

classroom applications of, 81–88

embedding tracking in curricula, 83–84

and headphones, 116

and helping students with dyslexia, 77–80

listening and tracking, differences between, 82–83

recording your textbook, 88

reproducibles for, 93–100

summary, 90–92

tracking traditions, starting, 86

what is tracking, 75–77

transformers, 153

U

understanding the impact of artificial intelligence. *See* artificial intelligence (AI)

using headphones as an educational support. *See* headphones, use of

using speech-to-text tools. *See* speech-to-text tools

using text-to-speech tools. *See* text-to-speech tools

V

Venger, I., 147, 148

videos. *See also* recorded lessons

as accommodations, 128

artificial intelligence and, 150

headphones and, 109

making your own videos, 87

recording devices for, 130–133

vocabulary

dyslexia and, 29–30

tracking with audio-assisted reading and, 78

vocabulary of AI, 151–153

Voice Dream Reader, 28, 32, 76–77. *See also* text-to-speech tools; tracking with audio-assisted reading

voice typing, use of term, 51

voice-to-text, use of term, 51

volume, 112, 118. *See also* headphones, use of

W

Wang, L., 108

Whitten, C., 111

wireless (Bluetooth) headphones, 105. *See also* headphones, use of

Y

Yeung, M., 151–152

Z

Zingoni, A., 155

The ADMIRE Framework for Inclusion
Toby J. Karten
Cultivate an environment that creates successful inclusion classrooms. Use this framework to help strengthen self-efficacy and accommodate students with diverse abilities. Dive into evidence-based practices and strategies to assess, delineate, model, instruct, reflect, and engage the skill sets of all learners.
BKG174

Watch, Listen, Ask, Learn
Belinda Dunnick Karge
Whether you're a superintendent or general education teacher leader, you can use this book to support inclusive education. Author Belinda Dunnick Karge offers research-based practices for implementing effective learning services based on sound knowledge of law and multitiered systems of supports (MTSS).
BKG080

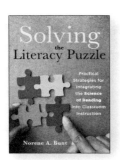

Solving the Literacy Puzzle
Norene A. Bunt
This book consolidates decades of research on effective literacy instruction. It provides a clear model for designing effective reading instruction that integrates the science of reading and evidence-based strategies. Teachers and educators can learn to confidently implement these strategies in the classroom.
BKG158

The Collaborative IEP
Kristen M. Bordonaro and Megan Clarke
Geared toward a collaborative approach, this book equips educators to write effective individualized education plans (IEPs). The authors break down IEPs to provide a practical working knowledge of how collaborative teams can create stronger IEPs, leading to more robust instruction and learning.
BKG122

Solution Tree | Press

Visit SolutionTree.com or call 800.733.6786 to order.

Quality team learning **from authors you trust**

Global PD Teams is the first-ever **online professional development resource designed to support your entire faculty on your learning journey.** This convenient tool offers daily access to videos, mini-courses, eBooks, articles, and more packed with insights and research-backed strategies you can use immediately.

GET STARTED
SolutionTree.com/**GlobalPDTeams**
800.733.6786